# CANTERBURY
## SUBURBS & SURROUNDINGS

T0386658

BRITAIN IN OLD PHOTOGRAPHS

# CANTERBURY
## SUBURBS & SURROUNDINGS

### PAUL CRAMPTON

*Frontispiece:* Canterbury firemen tackle a blaze at No. 9 St Stephen's Fields, during August 1956. In the middle distance, onlookers are standing in St Stephen's Pathway. Behind them is the upper garage of the East Kent Road Car Company. This scene is entirely lost today. Further pictures of this area can be found in Chapter 4.

Looking into the city from the grounds of St Edmund's School in the early 1950s. The top of St Thomas' Hill is just out of sight to the right. This area of suburban Canterbury is covered in Chapter 2.

First published 2010

The History Press
The Mill, Brimscombe Port
Stroud, Gloucestershire, GL5 2QG
www.thehistorypress.co.uk

British Library Cataloguing in Publication Data.
A catalogue record for this book is available from the British Library.

ISBN 978 0 7524 5572 3

Typesetting and origination by The History Press
Printed and bound by TJ International Ltd, Padstow, Cornwall

# CONTENTS

# ACKNOWLEDGEMENTS

Although many of the images used in this book have come from my own extensive archive, I would like to thank the following for kindly supplying additional photographs: *Kentish Gazette*, Derek Butler, Ben May, Harold Elsey, Barry Stretch, Clive Bowley, Barretts of Canterbury, John Clark, Ted Yeoman, Rob Williams, Dick Brown and Canterbury Museums.

I would also like to pay tribute to those photographers and contributors to this book who are no longer with us: Kenneth Gravett, Bill Entwhistle, Edward Wilmot and David Cousins.

The result of a two-vehicle collision on the old A2 at Upper Harbledown, during August 1957. The other vehicle, a car, came off considerably worse, as can be seen in Chapter 1. Today, this location is just beyond the car park of the former Wyevale garden centre.

# INTRODUCTION

This is the twelfth pictorial book I have compiled about Canterbury so far, but the very first one to exclusively dedicate itself to those parts of the city that lie outside of the defensive city wall circuit, i.e. extramural Canterbury. Although the familiar form of the cathedral may be glimpsed in the background of a number of photographs within these pages, I have resisted the temptation to stray too close, at least on this occasion. This policy has allowed me to concentrate on many areas of our suburbs in detail, as opposed to the usual cursory glance. For example, in this volume I have been able to study many streets in Northgate that have completely changed over the last fifty-odd years, largely for slum clearance. These lost, humble homes are rarely featured in local history books, but they can be found here, together with, in many cases, details of the people who once lived there. As such, *Canterbury Suburbs & Surroundings* can serve as a useful genealogical tool, as well as being, hopefully, a fascinating local and social history.

Most of Canterbury's suburbs have slowly grown up along the main trunk roads into the city, many being of Roman origin, or around churches and other religious foundations such as St Augustine's Abbey and St Gregory's Priory. However, for many centuries, much of extramural Canterbury was given over to farmland and market gardens, such as along Sturry Road, in south Canterbury and across much of Wincheap. Then, bit-by-bit, these agrarian centres became swallowed up by new development, as happened at Westgate Farm off London Road and St Lawrence Farm in south Canterbury. Others were converted to new uses like Beverley Farm off the main Whitstable Road.

Some suburbs became well-known in the medieval period for holding various types of market. Today, clues to these ancient uses can be found in their names, and also by the surviving broad swathes of street where the markets were once held. Good examples of both are at the Canterbury end of Wincheap, and in Longport to the south of the St Augustine's Abbey precinct.

The city suburbs began to expand significantly from the early nineteenth century onwards, largely with various forms of housing. Moreover, the type of house constructed, and the social classes for whom they were provided, tended to be concentrated in different parts of suburban Canterbury. Therefore, small military dwellings could be found almost exclusively in Northgate, with larger artisan houses in St Dunstan's and Wincheap, while the more prestigious 'villas' spread themselves along London Road and both New and Old Dover Roads. However, the smallest and most crowded tenements could still be found within the city walls, and would not be replaced until the first suburban council housing estates emerged in the late 1920s.

The 1942 blitz affected a number of suburbs, especially St Dunstan's, St Augustine's and across south-east Canterbury. And then, from the late 1950s onwards, slum clearance accounted for the loss of many old houses, and not just in Northgate. Post-war road widening also caused further demolition, often in the guise of slum clearance, to allow for the use of compulsory purchase under the 1955 Housing Act. Today, extramural Canterbury continues to change, and there will be ample scope for a second volume of *Suburbs & Surroundings* in the next couple of years.

A fascinating glimpse along part of the east side of Northgate, as it appeared in April 1961. None of these old houses survive today. This stretch of the street is considered in much more detail within Chapter 5.

The widening of Lower Chantry Lane in about 1955, as seen from the premises of Amey's Blinds in Ivy Lane. In the background are the Cooper Almshouses and, to the right, the terraced houses of Edward Road. Lower Chantry Lane is featured in Chapters 7 and 8.

# ❧ 1 ❧

# LONDON ROAD

The A2 London Road into Canterbury is one of the most historically significant approaches to the city, as it once formed part of the Roman 'Watling Street' from London to Dover. And then, in medieval times, it became the principal route by which pilgrims travelled to worship, or say penance, at the Becket shrine in Canterbury Cathedral. In its last few miles, the road passes through the former Victorian farming community of Upper Harbledown, before undulating its way through the ancient village of Harbledown. It then descends Summer Hill to the old city boundary before following a straight course, actually called 'London Road', and finally meeting the Whitstable Road on the outskirts of the St Dunstan's suburb. In 1085, Archbishop Lanfranc founded St Nicholas' Leper Hospital at Harbledown, and its largely unspoilt church can still be found there.

In much more recent times, the ever-increasing amount and size of motor vehicles has prompted new road construction along the London Road approaches to Canterbury. In 1963, the Rheims Way was opened, the section of it from Summer Hill to the St Peter's Place roundabout being an A2 diversion. Around ten years later, the village of Harbledown was bypassed to the north.

The twentieth century also saw a vast increase in the number of houses built adjacent to the A2 approach to the city. The London Road Estate was first established in the early 1950s. Originally conceived as the village of 'New Harbledown', the housing estate acquired its more generic name following a shifting of the city boundary, and the development's absorption into Canterbury proper.

The sad result of a fatal two-vehicle collision on the old A2 at Upper Harbledown, during August 1957. There is little left of the elderly pre-war Austin, which was heading in the Canterbury direction when it collided with a private operator's coach (see page 6). A policeman waits to direct traffic around the incident. In the distance, the A2 climbs towards the Gate Inn at Dunkirk. Such accidents only became more common during the 1960s and 1970s until the Canterbury bypass, the 'new' London Road, was finally completed.

After completion of the Canterbury bypass in the early 1980s, the village of Upper Harbledown became a much more pleasant place to live. Inevitably, new residential development followed, albeit limited by the area's recently won 'conservation area' status. In the picture, a Townscape scheme called Little Meadow is reaching an advanced stage of completion in June 1982. The new bypass resides in a cutting about 50 yards or so beyond the dense line of poplar trees in the background.

A by-now quiet part of the ancient village of Harbledown in the early 1980s, after the opening of the village bypass to the north in the early 1970s, and the larger Canterbury bypass to the south around ten years later. Gone are the coaches and articulated lorries that once sped around this tight bend. Only the crash barriers remain as a reminder of noisier, more dangerous times. Nearly thirty years later, this scene has changed remarkably little. Even the old K6 telephone box still survives *in situ*.

Nos 3 to 5 Summer Hill, also known as 'The Villas', as they were in 1941. This fine three-storey Regency terrace is more reminiscent of Kentish seaside resorts such as Broadstairs, than it is of the surroundings of Canterbury. At the time, the residents were as follows: Herbert Skelton and Jack Skelton – sanitary engineer (No. 3), Mrs F.M. Tritton (No. 4) and Paul Logan (No. 5). Again, the view has changed little during the intervening years.

*Left:* The old city boundary on the A2 approach to Canterbury on a cold-looking day in about 1951. This is also the point where Summer Hill becomes London Road. To the right, the newly constructed junction for Knight Avenue allows access into the London Road Estate, wehich was under construction at the time. The cathedral stands out well in the background, and across meadowland that would be swallowed up by the Rheims Way in the 1960s (see pages 14 and 15).

*Below:* The modernist-styled building of the new Frank Hooker Secondary School, taking shape in May 1955. This would become the crown jewel of the expanding London Road Estate, which would also account for much of its catchment area. Frank Hooker was a former Mayor of Canterbury who lived in London Road and donated the land to make this development possible. Today, the man's legacy is no longer acknowledged, and the school is known as Canterbury High.

The little Co-op, dedicated to the London Road Estate, shortly after completion and opening in 1953. It is situated at No. 3 Merchant's Way, and was first run by Cyril Tapsell. From new, this small shop also incorporated a post office. The estate also had its own dedicated pub in the form of the Gentil Knyght, opened a little later on in July 1958.

A huddle of council officials inspect a newly completed terrace of houses in November 1954. Unlike those built on the London Road Estate during its first phase, these particular houses were more experimental in nature, featuring, as they did, a number of pre-fabricated elements. Note the metal-sheet roofing. The City Council was rightly proud of their new London Road Estate houses, and hosted visits by government officials on more than one occasion.

A caravan rally situated on meadowland just off the London Road in the summer of 1954. To the far right is a row of trees that would mark the boundary of the proposed Frank Hooker School (see page 12). Far left, the semi-detached houses of the Queens Avenue, Crown Gardens and Princes Way development are currently under construction. Less than eight years later, this meadowland would be swallowed up by the city's new A2 bypass and first stage of the ring road, to be collectively known as the Rheims Way.

The aforementioned Rheims Way under construction in October 1962. The tarmac surfaces seem to have been completed but, as yet, the new dual carriageway has not been connected to the foot of Summer Hill, seen on the left. No roundabout was then being proposed for Knight Avenue, the main access road to the London Road Estate, nor would there be a pedestrian underpass. This meant that until both features finally came into being in about 1970, people and vehicles would have to cross the Rheims Way in two somewhat dangerous stages.

The slightly retrospective official opening of the Rheims Way in June 1963. In the centre is the mayor of the French city of Rheims (Canterbury's recently twinned city), Monsieur Taittinger, who pulls the cord to unveil the new sign. Far right, is the then Mayor of Canterbury, Cllr Ernest Kingsman. This ceremony was followed by a parade through the city, speeches by all concerned and, of course, an elaborate lunch.

The many seated and elaborately-hatted guests invited to witness the official opening ceremony for Rheims Way, in June 1963. In truth, many of these people would already have been able to use the new road for a few weeks. Behind, the standing 'uninvited' guests also look on with interest. In the background are the houses of Knight Avenue and Mill Lane, being part of the London Road Estate.

Firemen tackle a blazing barn on the east side of London Road during the morning of 22 January 1944. This was caused by an incendiary bomb, dropped during the very last enemy raid on Canterbury of the Second World War. The barn was part of Burton's Farm, also known as Westgate Farm, which occupied much land in this area until the early post-war years. The final raid of January 1944 also almost completely destroyed the garage and showrooms of Barrett's Motors in St Peter's Street.

A section of London Road looking away from the city, on a grey, wintry day in about 1953. On the left, a new road to be called Princes Way has recently been laid across the site of the lost barn of Burton's Farm. New semi-detached houses would soon be built along its length (see page 14). This photograph must have been taken at either the very beginning or end of the day, as neither vehicle nor person can be seen.

St Dunstan's Church of England School on the east side of London Road, January 1957. Interestingly, the 1955 *Kelly's Street Directory* lists it as a secondary modern school, although it had certainly become a primary school by the time I first attended in 1964. The school has since closed and been converted for residential use. All the buildings, except the pre-fabricated 'ministry hut', survive today.

An early 1950s view of the west side of London Road, at the city end. This row of seventeenth-century Georgian and Regency houses will be familiar to local people today, although the four humbler houses at the far end may not. These are, or were, Nos 16 to 19 London Road, the 1952 residents being Mrs F.A. Epps (No. 16), Ernest Baxter (No. 17), Peter Hadley (No. 18) and John Goldsack (No. 20). This terrace of four houses disappeared in the late 1950s, to be replaced by the new St Dunstan's Close, and a pair of semi-detached houses.

*Left:* Queens Avenue in April 1953, looking towards the Regency houses of St Dunstan's Terrace. At the time, the land to the left was still open having once been part of Westgate Farm, but new semi-detached houses would be built here within a year. The far end of St Dunstan's Terrace joins London Road adjacent to the St Dunstan's School (see page 17).

*Below:* Running parallel to St Dunstan's Terrace is New Street, and off New Street is a short cul-de-sac known as Ryde Street. The picture, from a 1937 survey, shows the fronts of Nos 11 to 14 Ryde Street, being part of a group of small tenements also once known as Grove Place. They are probably of late eighteenth- or early nineteenth-century date. The 1937 *Kelly's* shows the properties as empty, but someone must still have been in residence, hence the socks on the line, and the rather contented-looking cat! These tenements were demolished in 1938 and today a single modern house stands on the site.

# ❦ 2 ❦

# WHITSTABLE ROAD

The main route from Whitstable passes through the hamlet of Pean Hill, and then the village of Blean before skimming the edge of Rough Common. It finally descends on St Thomas' Hill and approaches the city from the north-west. Anciently, the road was used to bring salt from Seasalter and fish from Whitstable into Canterbury, alongside certain quantities of smuggled goods! There were no medieval religious foundations on the Whitstable approach to Canterbury, but the nineteenth century saw the establishment of prestigious educational centres on either side of the top part of St Thomas' Hill in the form of St Edmund's School and Kent College. The area's reputation as a hub of learning was further enhanced by the opening of the University of Kent, just off St Thomas' Hill, in 1965. The hill itself once descended towards the city along an ancient hollow way, part of which still survives immediately to the south-west of the present road. The final stretch of the Whitstable Road, as it approaches the St Dunstan's suburb, is actually named as such. This section was developed for residential use in the Regency period, with further building phases in the 1920s and 1930s. Forty Acres Road, which links the village of Hackington with the suburb of St Dunstan's, is also included in this chapter.

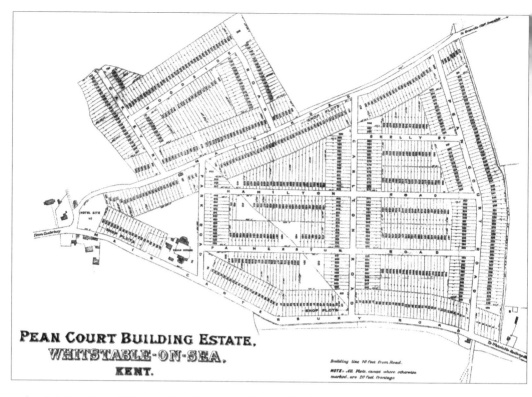

PEAN COURT BUILDING ESTATE,
WHITSTABLE-ON-SEA,
KENT.

Building line 10 feet from Road.
NOTE: All Plots, except where otherwise
marked, are 20 feet frontage

A detailed plan from 1900 showing the proposed layout for the new Pean Court Building Estate between Whitstable and Blean. The scheme would have transformed Pean Hill from a linear hamlet on the Whitstable to Canterbury road into a small new town. In the plan, the main A290 runs along the bottom, and the diagonal 'Main Road' follows the route of Fox's Cross Road. In the event, much of the road plan was laid out and a few houses built, but the scheme had petered out by the outbreak of the First World War. Today, some of the planned roads still exist as farm tracks or unmetalled lanes.

Part of the village of Blean on the A290 Whitstable Road in the late 1940s. In the foreground is Blean Hill and climbing up the other side is Tile Kiln Hill. The photographer is looking in the Canterbury direction. Note the telegraph poles with their many porcelain insulators. At the bottom of the hill, to the left, is the Hare & Hounds pub, and at the top of the far hill, also on the left, is Blean Primary School.

An aerial view of part of the village of Rough Common, some time in the early 1930s. In the foreground is Ravenscourt Road, and at the top left, the Rough Common Road itself. At this time, many of these houses had only recently been built, and some can clearly be seen still in the course of construction. In the early post-war years, further housing would be constructed across much of the remaining nursery-style farmland seen here.

The boarded-up and abandoned 'mystery house', as the *Kentish Gazette* reported it at the time, standing at the far end of Ross Gardens on a snowy day in January 1971. The building would soon be demolished and replaced by a modern house set further back on the same plot. In more recent years, the 'mystery' of this building's history and purpose has been solved. It had once been the Woodreeve's Cottage for nearby Church Wood (the woodreeve is effectively the woodland manager and overseer) and the house is reputed to have been built in 1649.

The Gothic revival buildings of St Edmund's School, as seen from Giles Lane in 1950. The main Whitstable Road is just beyond the buildings to the right. At this time, the headmaster was Mr M.A. Thoseby. Originally conceived as the Clergy Orphan College, the complex was finally finished in 1857, when the chapel was constructed. Today, a section of the mid-Victorian school is obscured by a modernist brick extension, completed in 1968.

The top and level section of St Thomas' Hill on a summer's day sometime in 1948. This picture was part of a survey of this part of the Whitstable road, commissioned by the city engineer prior to road improvements. St Edmund's School is out of sight behind the shrubs and trees to the right. Left, by the bus stop, is the junction of Elm Grove, leading into Neal's Place Road, followed by the grounds of Kent College. A single car interrupts this otherwise traffic-free scene.

Another photograph from the city engineer's 1948 survey, this time looking down St Thomas' Hill and towards the city. Once again, a solitary vehicle, a small lorry in this case, is the only visible traffic. Also note another example of the old-style telegraph poles. Far below, the city simmers in a heat haze, although the cathedral stands out well. Just out of sight, to the right, is the City of Canterbury pub. In the early 1960s, the new University Road would be constructed to the left.

The aforementioned City of Canterbury public house, an un-numbered property on the south-west side of St Thomas' Hill, in 1965. It dates from the early nineteenth century and was probably purpose-built as a pub. In the early to mid-1960s, University Road was constructed opposite the City of Canterbury. And then, when the pub closed in 1971, it was converted into student accommodation. Today, the building is a bed-and-breakfast establishment, with a slightly altered front elevation.

Beverley Farm, captured during a stroll on a winter's day in 1899. The farmhouse, of undoubted medieval origin, is perched atop the sloping ground to the north-west of Canterbury, and situated about half-a-mile from St Thomas' Hill. Access to the farm could be gained via a long track that wandered up from the outskirts of the city, beginning at the end of what would become Salisbury Road (see page 56). The turn-of-the-century occupant of Beverley Farm was Mrs Hawkins, with Mr John Green as bailiff.

The front of Beverley Farmhouse, as recorded in the early 1960s, during the final years of agricultural use. A large wing, added in the Edwardian period, can be seen on the left. When the new University of Kent authorities took over the area in December 1963, this was the only habitable building on the site. Even so, the former farmhouse had to be abandoned in the 1970s, due to poor state of repair. Full restoration followed in 1985.

The first part of a panoramic view of the city, taken from the fields of Beverley Farm, probably in about 1900. Beyond the fields are the greenhouses of Mount's Rose Nursery in Forty Acres Road (see page 27). Further away are the oast houses off Hanover Road (to be renamed Roper Road in the wave of anti-German feeling during the First World War) and the houses and warehouses of Station Road West (see page 36). The cathedral stands out particularly well in this view.

The second part of the 1900 panoramic view clearly shows the then limit of residential development along the Whitstable Road (bottom right). In the centre are the Westgate Towers, which appear to be flying a rather large Union Flag. Spread out in front of the city gate is the suburb of St Dunstan's, which will be extensively featured in the following chapter. Also note the thin spire of the now-lost church of St Mary Bredin on the far right (see page 113).

*Left:* A fascinating group of late eighteenth- and early nineteenth-century houses on the south-west side of Whitstable Road at the 'Canterbury end' on 17 May 1953. Featured, from left to right, are Nos 11 to 27 (odds only). The then residents were as follows: E. Beasley & Son, dyers (11); Ronald Bean (13); Archibald Field (15); Sidney Baker (17); Miss Fearn (19); Mrs H. Clark, grocers (21 & 23); Miss A. Philpott (25) and Thomas Pearson (27). Nos 17 and 19 would later be demolished and replaced by a pair of flats. The shop fell victim to the latest round of post office closures.

*Below:* Diagonally opposite the group of buildings referred to above is the junction of Forty Acres Road. Just up on the east side could once be found this corrugated-iron building, photographed here in 1987. It had existed since at least 1910, when it was part of the premises for Solly and Vane, fly proprietors (a fly being a small single-horse-drawn carriage). By 1937, it had become part of St Dunstan's Garage, run by Mr H.A. Solly. Note the tower of St Dunstan's Church in the background, together with the ancient roofs of buildings in Whitstable Road (see page 28).

Another part of the former garage in Forty Acres Road, near the more recently created Roseacre Close (left). This brick building was, in fact, the truncated remains of a larger Victorian-period house, set in the corner of a large garden plot. What fate befell the house is unknown, but Solly and Vane would later rebuild what was left of it, and also erect the corrugated-iron building in the former garden area. In the 1960s, the buildings became Canterbury Auto Electrical Ltd. They were finally demolished for residential redevelopment of the site shortly after the pictures were taken in 1987.

The mid-section of Forty Acres Road, looking away from the Whitstable Road junction, March 1967. To the right is the junction into Beverley Road. On the left is the hedge that marks the boundary of G. Mount & Sons Ltd, nursery & wholesale florists. By the late 1960s, Mount's many square feet of greenhouses had been cleared away prior to residential development of the whole area.

The north side of Whitstable Road, beyond Forty Acres Road, in about 1949. This section stretches down into St Dunstan's Street, with the junction for London Road off to the right. On the left, Nos 2 to 6 Whitstable Road (evens only) are featured. The 1949 residents were as follows: Henry Solly (2), Albert Lawson (4) and Miss Nash (6). In the early 1960s, No. 2 was converted into a hairdressers shop. Further down can be seen The Monument public house, at the top end of St Dunstan's Street.

A similar view to the one at the top of the page, but seen in the opposite direction, some time in the early 1950s. The photographer is standing at the top end of St Dunstan's Street, with London Road veering off to the left, and Whitstable Road extending away to the right. Nos 2 to 8 Whitstable Road are on the far right, followed by the junction to Forty Acres Road. This scene has changed very little in the last fifty-odd years, except it would be almost impossible to photograph a largely traffic-free view these days.

# ❦ 3 ❦

# ST DUNSTAN'S

The suburb of St Dunstan's has always had an individual character of its own. This is largely due to the presence of the city gate, the Westgate, which has become an effective 'barrier' between the suburb and the main intramural part of Canterbury. And remember, the Westgate was closed at night, thus emphasising the division. This also meant that any late-arriving pilgrims would have to find board and lodging in St Dunstan's, hence the establishment of inns such as the Falstaff in the late-medieval period. The suburb's principal religious building, St Dunstan's Church, is well known for two main reasons. Firstly, it was here in 1174 that Henry II rested a while and prepared himself for a painful penance at the tomb of his former friend, Thomas Becket, in Canterbury Cathedral. Secondly, placed in a wall niche within the burial vault of the Tudor-period Roper Chapel is the severed head of Sir (or Saint) Thomas More, its crumbling remains housed within a split lead casket. His daughter, Margaret Roper (who had married into a Canterbury Catholic family), rescued his head from its pike atop London Bridge and brought it back to the family home in St Dunstan's Street. The only surviving part of the Roper mansion is the magnificent gateway, which still fronts onto St Dunstan's Street today (see page 31). The nineteenth century saw great change in St Dunstan's, principally its bisection by the arrival of the South Eastern Railway. Even today, the level crossing significantly affects the progress of both pedestrians and vehicles along St Dunstan's Street at all times.

As mentioned in the London Road chapter, the last enemy raid on Canterbury occurred in the small hours of 22 January 1944. This picture shows firemen examining the gutted remains of Swoffer & Co., fruit merchants at No. 46 St Dunstan's Street. To the left, the ancient cottage at No. 47, the home of Mrs Collins, has become a victim of the same incendiary bomb. Damaged but salvageable is No. 48 (far left), the confectioner's shop run by Thomas Chantler.

The same section of the south side of St Dunstan's Street, in about 1952. Swoffer's had rebuilt their premises in an art deco style during the late 1940s. The gutted cottage at No. 47 was not rebuilt, its position being marked by the walled-off gap in the building line. Left is the repaired confectioner and newsagent shop, by then being run by Mrs F. Chantler. Far left is a similar terraced cottage of probable seventeenth-century date, then the home of Claude Ware (No. 49). The little general shop still survives today, whereas the former Swoffer's warehouse was demolished in 1987 for residential redevelopment.

The Roper Gate on the north side of St Dunstan's Street, photographed in August 1957. This is surely one of Canterbury's most famous Tudor structures. For many years, it had been incorporated into the buildings of the Fremlins Brewery (No. 33), but it had recently been closed and at the time this picture was taken, the buildings were currently waiting to be re-let as industrial premises. To the right, one of the former brewery chimneys is being dismantled brick-by brick. This well-known gate once gave access to the Roper family's house, of which nothing now remains.

A summer fête in the back garden of Roper House in June 1959. This large, elegant property stands slightly further up on the north side of St Dunstan's Street from the old brewery building, and may occupy the site of the lost Tudor house of the same name. Once a private dwelling itself, the current Roper House had become the Royal National Institute for the Deaf by the mid-1950s. In the picture, gleeful girls try to dislodge a bucket of water onto their doubtless stoic victim.

A large section of the south side of St Dunstan's Street in 1941. Far right is the then intact Swoffer premises, followed by the old cottages at Nos 47 to 50 (see page 30). Next comes the junction for Orchard Street. After that is No. 51, right down to the two-storey house at No. 60, on the far left. Of particular interest are the houses of Nos 56 to 59 (centre left). The steeply pitched roofline gives away the sixteenth- or early seventeenth-century origins of these largely timber-framed buildings. The addition of later 'Georgianised' frontages, as seen here, was a common practice in Canterbury.

The west corner of the junction of Orchard Street with St Dunstan's Street in 1965. Advertising posters plaster the remaining ground-floor walls of the former three-storey house at No. 50 (also visible in the top picture). This house had been empty since the outbreak of the Second World War and was probably partly demolished sometime in the early 1950s. Next door, No. 49 stands empty, rather derelict and itself awaiting demolition (see page 30). Just visible, far right, is once again the confectioner-newsagents at No. 48, now being run by Mr D.J. Hatt.

The east corner of the Orchard Street junction in about 1967. Prominent is the family butcher's shop of H.M. Marsh at Nos 51 and 52 St Dunstan's Street. As far back as the Edwardian era, this place had been a butcher's shop. In 1910 it was being run by Mr A.W. Clark and, in the Second World War, by Herbert Rigden.

The same scene a few months later, after the shop had been converted into a new branch for the Westminster Bank. Gone is the oriel window on the St Dunstan's Street frontage, and behind, in Orchard Street, the old rear extension has been entirely replaced. Far right is the weed-choked site of No. 50 St Dunstan's Street. This is now a hard-standing area. The bank remains in business today.

The imposing Railway Buildings on the north side of St Dunstan's Street between the junction of Roper Road (far left) and the railway crossing. This place had once been a school and, before that, a gaol. However, by 1941 it had been divided into four dwellings. The then residents were Frank Willes (1), Mrs M. Austen (2), Mrs M.E. Marsh (3) and George Jenkins (4). Note the absence of doorways along the St Dunstan's Street frontage. Railway Buildings were damaged in the June 1942 blitz, and demolished shortly afterwards. Far right is the premises of Edward Lee, antique dealer (No. 28). This was also lost as a result of war damage.

The empty site once occupied by Railway Buildings and Edward Lee's place, in about 1967. All that remains is a short wall fragment that once formed part of the antique shop. I clearly remember this empty, overgrown site in the 1960s, which had become a dumping ground for many old cars – a fascinating subject for small boys! In the early 1970s, the National Tyre Centre established a business here. Their brutalist building was demolished in 2008, and the site is once again empty, with residential redevelopment pending.

A wonderful panoramic view of the lower section of St Dunstan's Street in July 1954, as seen from the overgrown site featured on the opposite page. Note the old-style level crossing gates that would remain in use for many years to come. Today's faster automatic barriers still cause much disruption, due to an increase in road traffic rather than there being more trains. In fact, the number of freight trains traversing this line is now negligible since the closure of the Kent coalfield in the 1980s. Beyond the crossing are the many wonderful jettied and gabled buildings of the street's lower south side.

An unfortunate railway mishap across the complex of points between St Dunstan's level crossing and Canterbury West station in November 1958. It would appear that the station's 'top brass' have come out to inspect the scene. Later, a large steam crane would be summoned from Ashford to help restore order. Note the semaphore signals, water tower and loading gauge to the right, all now features of the past.

The junction of Station Road West from St Dunstan's Street in about 1910: a fascinating lost scene. To the left is an 1890s development of three-storey shops; at Nos 1 to 11 (odds only) Station Road West, these featured Court & Son, pianoforte tuners (No. 3) and the London Restaurant, run by Walter Targett (No. 5). On the right are the old Canterbury Baths, run by Walter Cozens, in a building that also encompassed the proprietor's own small museum. In the distance is Canterbury West station, the only building that survives from this old photograph today.

Roughly the same scene, on the morning of 1 June 1942. A combination of incendiary and high-explosive bombs has reduced the 1890s row of shops to a few tottering walls and stark chimney stacks. Opposite, Walter Cozens' place has been reduced to a pile of smouldering timbers. There had been some damage at this junction in an earlier enemy raid during September 1940, but now the destruction was complete. In both raids, the target was likely to have been the nearby Canterbury West station's coal and freight yard (see page 39), but this survived unscathed on both occasions.

Ten years on, and the site once occupied by those late Victorian three-storey shops is now a filling station and garage, run by Marcel Hallet. He also had a motorcycle shop at No. 26 St Dunstan's Street, situated between the new garage site and the level crossing. Further down Station Road West, to the right of the picture, are Nos 1 to 8 Station Cottages (see also page 38), built in the 1840s for the railway labour force as the new main line from Ashford arrived in the city.

The first of Hallet's new garage and showroom buildings, as seen from St Dunstan's Street on 14 November 1954. Another new building would later be constructed in the vacant space to the left. Seen on the far left is part of the butcher's shop of Ernest Hedger. This fine establishment is still there to this very day, and I would highly recommend their pork and sage sausages! Hallet's garage is no longer there however, and their former buildings, currently given over to other uses, are due to be demolished for a housing scheme.

*Above:* Southern 'N' class locomotive No. 31854 simmers at the Down platform of Canterbury West station with a stopping train to Margate. It is 1961, the last year of full steam operation on this particular line. As can be seen, the electric 'third rail' is already *in situ*, thus spelling the imminent end for such splendid steam locomotives. The two central through-lines, seen in the foreground, would last until January 1979.

*Left:* Station Cottages, off Station Road West, in July 1974, just after a group of well-meaning squatters had been evicted from No. 3. However, their banner, which reads 'Homes for people, not for profit', is still defiantly displayed. This sturdy terrace of eight cottages had been specially built by the South Eastern Railway for their local work force, and could by no means be described as slums. Sadly, demolition occurred shortly after this picture was taken.

A panoramic view of the west side of Station Road West in June 1978. The surviving rear ground-floor walls of the demolished Station Cottages can be seen in the middle distance, close to the railway perimeter fence. Also, note the railway oil depot, on the other side of then main line, which saw regular diesel-hauled trains throughout the 1970s and 1980s. This bramble-choked Station Road West site would finally be laid out as a pay-and-display car park in the mid-1980s, some ten years after the cottages had been removed.

This view, from a few hundred yards further along the line, dates from August 1986 and shows the rusting and weed-strewn lines of the old West Station coal yard fanning out from the main line. Even at this late stage, the yard saw the occasional train, albeit for temporary storage. Today, the extension to Station Road West runs across where the coal yard tracks once existed. The long, single-storey building is also no longer there, but the well-known signal-box still spans the main line today.

The famous Falstaff Hotel on the north side of St Dunstan's Street, as seen in 1941. The photograph was part of an extensive survey jointly undertaken by the Fisk-Moore studios and the *Kent Messenger*. The aim was to have a record of Canterbury's more notable buildings, should they be lost in any subsequent bombing. Note the open coaching (or by then) car park entrance. Today, this has been blocked off to form the hotel's reception area. Also note the concrete cylinders (left), which were part of the city's invasion defences. They would be moved to form a barrier across the street should the worst happen.

As mentioned earlier in this chapter, bombing took place near the Station Road West junction in the autumn of 1940, and then again, more extensively on 1 June 1942. Rebuilding began in 1954 with the new garage and showroom for Hallet's (see page 37), and this new shop building to the east of the Kirby's Lane junction. The latter is pictured here on 14 November 1954. The first occupants were M.S. Benjamin, tailor (17), on the right and Wheatley's tobacconist (18) to the left.

The picturesque setting of Westgate Grove from across Westgate Gardens, as part of the 1941 survey. The vehicle to the right is in the process of removing the garden's iron railings for war salvage. On the corner with St Dunstan's Street (right) is the Riverside Commercial Hotel and café, run by Mr S.A. Causton. Today, the trees have gone, as has the three-storey building (far right) on the opposite side of St Dunstan's Street. This was Kennett & Sons Depository which was damaged in the 1942 blitz and pulled down completely by the end of the decade.

A smartly turned-out army cadet band waits in Westgate Grove on 24 October 1954, prior to taking part in a parade to commemorate United Nations Day. The buildings of Westgate Grove are also smartly turned-out, ready to provide the subject for many a tourist camera. Far right, the hotel and café has now become Ben Lee's antique shop, which was familiar to many of us who grew up in 1950s and 1960s Canterbury. Today, it is the excellent Café des Amis Mexican restaurant.

A 1952 picture, taken from Westgate Gardens, and looking towards North Lane from across the River Stour and also St Dunstan's Street. The removal of Kennett's Depository, seen on the previous page, has made this view possible. Note the tall chimneys and roofs of the buildings on the east side of North Lane. Also note the two telephone boxes, which have since been re-sited on the opposite side of the main street.

A panoramic view of much of North Lane, as seen from atop the Westgate in 1956. The tall-chimneyed buildings, seen in the top picture, have been demolished and reduced to piles of rubble (bottom right). However, of special interest is the as-yet almost completely unbroken line of buildings on the west side of North Lane, with one of the East Kent bus garages (see page 45) and the railway coal yard behind them.

Another 1956 picture of North Lane, but this time taken from ground level and looking towards the Westgate and St Dunstan's Street. The rubble of the recently demolished buildings, on the street's east side, can once again be seen. Also apparent in this view is the considerable narrowing of North Lane along this section, a problem that would soon be cured as a result of the aforementioned demolition. Premises lost during the clearance included those for William Buddle, blacksmith (No. 51), and the hairdresser's shop of Ernest Flower (No. 52).

Returning to the west side of North Lane, and a picture taken in 1964. By this time, the bus company had bought up many of the old cottages immediately in front of their heavy engineering garage and were gradually demolishing them to provide additional space. In this view, three withdrawn buses are parked on the site of a recently pulled-down three-storey, jettied house of seventeenth-century date, which is just visible in the picture opposite. The city council strongly objected to this policy, as they wanted the charm of these old cottages to be enjoyed by traffic speeding along the proposed ring road opposite, a project that itself would cause much demolition!

*Above:* An early post-war view of the Blue Anchor pub, to be found further along the west side of North Lane. At this time, it was being run by Joseph Shaw. Left is the narrow opening that leads to Blue Anchor Passage where two small tenements could once be found. To the right is the warehouse of Kennett & Sons (No. 26), converted from an early post-medieval timber-framed house by the removal of its entire frontage. Today, the pub is a restaurant, and the former warehouse has been fully restored with a rebuilt façade.

*Left:* To the right of the Blue Anchor and old warehouse were further cottages, which had also been bought up by East Kent buses. These two-storey dwellings were of probable late sixteenth- or early seventeenth-century date. Inevitably, these cottages were progressively pulled down by the bus company, this time in the 1950s. The picture, dating from 12 November 1954, shows one of the old properties, probably No. 28, being stripped prior to demolition. Today, the site has been redeveloped for housing, as a facsimile of those cottages lost in the 1950s.

A wider view of this section of North Lane from 1966, by which time the bus company had demolished many of the old cottages along the lane's frontage, despite the city council's protestations. The Blue Anchor pub can once again be seen to the left; it would finally close as a hostelry in 1971. Just visible to the right is a small garage and filling station on the east side of North Lane, being part of the Bligh Bros empire. A further picture of these premises can be found overleaf.

The frontage of the East Kent Road Car Company engineering works in North Lane, just after closure in the late 1980s. Access to the forecourt could be gained just to the left of the Blue Anchor, seen in the top picture. These purpose-built premises, which extended right back to Kirby's Lane, first appeared in 1920. Demolition occurred in the mid-1990s, prior to residential development of the entire area.

Derelict and boarded-up cottages on the east side of North Lane in June 1976. They had been doomed by the proposed third and final stage of the city ring road, but this missing link had finally been cancelled in October 1975. These houses would subsequently be renovated, and returned to residential use. To the left is the small Bligh Bros garage, seen on the previous page and also below.

The former Bligh's premises in North Lane, during its last days in the mid-1980s – it would soon be demolished for a retirement development. It is hard to believe that in the mid-1960s this garage courted national controversy by employing bikini-clad girls on the small filling station forecourt. It wasn't long before the television cameras arrived! Subsequently, Bligh Bros reverted to offering green stamps as the only customer inducement.

# ❦ 4 ❦

# ST STEPHEN'S HACKINGTON

The St Stephen's suburb, as we know it today, has grown out from the medieval village of Hackington. At the heart of the original community is St Stephen's Church. Interestingly, this is partly built from stonework salvaged from an earlier religious building (possibly the cathedral) following the 'great fire' of 1174, and the subsequent reconstruction of its eastern arm. Another notable aspect of St Stephen's Church is the impressive tomb of Sir Roger Manwood, whose Tudor-brick almshouses still front the village green today. Another significant Hackington building, now lost, was 'Place House', a vast mansion that once stood on the site now occupied by the playing field in front of the church. Place House was only pulled down once its replacement had been completed. This was the imposing mid-eighteenth-century house known as 'Hales Place'. Sadly demolished in 1928, Hales Place became a quarry for thousands of bricks used to build many of the suburb's houses throughout the 1930s. In 1955, Canterbury's weekly livestock market moved to the suburb on a purpose-built site along Market Way. Also in the 1950s, and through into the 1960s, many hundreds of houses were constructed in the expanding suburb, partly prompting the extension of Beaconsfield Road to connect with St Stephen's Hill and thus improving communications in the area.

*Left:* Nos 8 and 9 St Stephen's Fields in a derelict state during October 1961. St Stephen's Fields was a curious L-shaped block of nine mainly nineteenth-century houses, in a variety of architectural styles. In 1961, four of the houses were still occupied, and by 1964 this had gone up to six. However, Nos 8 and 9 were never inhabited again. Indeed, during August 1956, No. 9 (left) had been damaged in a fire (see page 2). There was another separate building in St Stephen's Fields at the time, being the Barretts Radio Repair Dept at No. 10, situated in a former mineral water factory.

*Below:* A fascinating view of the city end of St Stephen's Pathway in March 1967. An ancient right-of-way, this path still links Canterbury with the ancient village of Hackington, albeit in a different guise. Seen left is No. 4 St Stephen's Pathway, one of a terrace of four cottages that also still survive today. Centre view is No. 1 St Stephen's Fields, part of the same block featured in the top picture, and then only a year from demolition. Centre right is Pinnock Ltd, coal merchant, and far right is the edge of East Kent's St Stephen's Road depot.

Another view of the end of St Stephen's Pathway, but this time looking towards the right. East Kent's St Stephen's Road bus depot is seen here in 1987. It was built in 1948 to replace an earlier version that had been damaged in a raid during September 1940, and then completely destroyed in the main Baedeker raid of 1 June 1942. This depot mainly concerned itself with bodywork and panelling repairs whereas heavier engineering was based at the North Lane works (see page 45).

The St Stephen's Road bus depot being pulled down in April 1996, thus ending East Kent's seventy-year occupation of the site. 1996 was a year of great change for this part of Canterbury as also demolished were East Kent's North Lane works and the former premises of both Pinnock's and Barretts, as mentioned on the opposite page. A vast residential development followed and the city end of St Stephen's Pathway has since been superseded by a new road linking St Stephen's Road with an extended Station Road West (see page 39).

The well-known timber-framed building 'Kingsmead House' pictured on 4 July 1954. Situated on the east side of St Stephen's Road, it proudly bears the date of 1620. Back in 1941 the place was divided into two dwellings, standing empty and being offered for sale together with three adjoining cottages of eighteenth-century date. Demolition was even threatened but in the event the seventeenth-century section was salvaged and restored. Beyond the gap (created by the loss of the three eighteenth-century houses) are Nos 80 and 82 St Stephen's Road, two large sixteenth-century timber-framed houses with a brick façade later erected in 1754.

Another view of Nos 80 and 82 St Stephen's Road, now seen from the rear, and looking across a branch of the River Stour. By 1955, when this picture was taken, the houses had been standing empty for some time and were in a dangerous state of collapse, as is evident by the need for shoring-up. The later street-side brick façade, however, was still in apparent good condition. Nevertheless, demolition occurred shortly after this photograph was taken. Modern semi-detached houses were subsequently built on the site.

The St Stephen's Maltings, situated at the end of Malthouse Road which runs off St Stephen's Road roughly opposite the buildings seen on the previous page. They had been built by brewers Mackeson & Co. during 1899 and 1900. The picture dates from 1966, shortly after purchase by Barretts. The new owners were responsible for inserting the windows along the south-facing elevation, but they also had to remove all the internal equipment associated with the process of making malt from barley, before occupation was possible. Barretts still trade from this site today.

The double-fronted Edwardian house at No. 23 St Stephen's Road standing at the corner with Malthouse Road. The house had long been converted into flats but by 1988, when this picture was taken, it was empty and suffering from significant structural failure, similar to the houses opposite over thirty years before. No. 23 was demolished later that year to provide an extended hard-standing area for Barretts.

An impressive line of period vehicles just off Market Way, shortly after the opening of the new Cattle Market in March 1955. Canterbury's livestock market had long-since been held on a purpose-built site off Upper Bridge Street and in the shadow of the city wall. However, it had been moved to its new site in the St Stephen's area, not least in order to make way for the city's proposed ring road.

Another view of the cattle market during the first week of operations in March 1955. Note the exclusively male clientele. Also note the row of small single-storey shops, occupied by those Canterbury firms who wanted a presence at the new cattle market. There was even a small pub – that is once the problem of obtaining a liquor licence had been sorted out. The area is now entirely redeveloped for housing, the last vestige of the market finally disappearing a few years ago when the former Farmer's Union office was demolished.

The crossing keeper's cottage at the St Stephen's Road level crossing in about 1967. It stood on the north side of the railway line and west of the road itself. Dating from the 1840s or 1850s, it was built by the South Eastern Railway to a standard pattern. Other similar former crossing keeper's cottages can still be found along the line, but this one at St Stephen's Road had gone by the end of the 1960s. Another, at the Broad Oak level crossing, was pulled down in January 1981 after a vehicle had collided with it.

The delightful Glebe Cottage on St Stephen's Green, photographed by Fisk-Moore as part of the 1941 survey. The green, now much reduced, was once at the heart of the ancient village of Hackington. There had also been a village pond here in medieval times, but bungalows now occupy the (hopefully) dried-up site. Glebe Cottage itself gives all the appearance of having originated as a Wealden hall, and could date back to as early as the fourteenth century. The track on the right once gave access to Beverley Dairy Farm, but now forms the Hackington end of St Stephen's Pathway (see page 48).

Sir Roger Manwood's Hospital or, as they are more popularly known, Manwood Almshouses, probably also taken as part of the 1941 building survey. Constructed in the 1570s by the aforementioned Sir Roger on St Stephen's Green, the hospital consists of six brick-built, two-storey cottages, plus a larger house at the far end. Originally, the larger dwelling was provided for the warden of the hospital, but for many years now, if not centuries, it has been Ye Olde Beverlie Inn. In 1941, the proprietor of the pub was Frank Wilson.

A fascinating aerial view of the former Hales Place mansion and later St Mary's College, in about 1927. By this time, all hope of selling the estate as a going concern had faded and, within a year, the buildings would be sold for their materials and demolished. From about 1930 onwards, houses began to appear across the mansion's grounds, although the intention was always to retain the eighteenth-century hard landscaping around the emerging development. The lost house's drive and front terrace were also retained and absorbed into the street pattern for the new scheme.

A survivor of the Hales Place 1928 clearance is this little chapel, still to be found at the bottom of Tenterden Drive. It is pictured here in the spring of 1955, prior to restoration by Anthony Swaine and Christopher Buckingham. Originally built as a dovecote, it became a chapel during the time of Mary Hales in the mid-nineteenth century. And then, in 1928, when the Catholic church (once associated with both the former mansion and the later college) was demolished, the principal burials from both eras were exhumed and re-buried in a circular pattern around this tiny building.

Looking down Tenterden Drive, on the Hales Place housing estate, during a massive building phase in January 1957. The tiny chapel featured at the top of the page is hidden in the clump of trees at the bottom of the slope (far right). The new houses emerging at this time were part of a plan that would see areas zoned for private development and others designated for council housing, those visible here being part of the latter scheme.

Beaconsfield Road, photographed as part of a housing survey in March 1967. Originally, Beaconsfield Road was a short cul-de-sac off Salisbury Road, which itself was a 1900s development along a footpath leading north out of the city. Then, in the late 1920s, Forty Acres Road was extended to connect with it, as part of a housing scheme (see page 27). Finally, in 1966, Beaconsfield Road itself was extended eastwards to connect with St Stephen's Hill. Removal of part of the embankment to the former Canterbury to Whitstable Railway made this last road scheme possible.

Nos 1 to 9 (odds only) Beaconsfield Road, near the junction with Salisbury Road (left), in March 1967. When the final road connection was made in 1966, the original short stretch of Beaconsfield Road became part of a busy through road. Unfortunately, the Edwardian period houses on the west side created a traffic pinch, as can be seen in the top picture. Complete demolition was considered but in the end only Nos 1 to 9 were condemned. They are seen here boarded up and awaiting the bulldozer. An improved junction into Salisbury Road also resulted.

# ❧ 5 ❧

# NORTHGATE

The suburb of Northgate first properly came into being during the early medieval period, establishing itself on either side of the old Roman road from Canterbury to Reculver and Thanet. The road entered the city via the North Gate, which had been established as far back as the third century and lasted until about 1830. Two religious houses were founded in Northgate, not long after the Norman Conquest. These were St John's Hospital on the road's west side, and St Gregory's Priory directly opposite it. Both were the inspiration of Archbishop Lanfranc and appeared in the 1080s. Whereas much of St John's Hospital still survives today, the last traces of St Gregory's Priory disappeared in the 1840s. Another ancient Northgate thoroughfare is Ruttington Lane which wrapped itself round the precincts of St Gregory's Priory. Much later, around the beginning of the nineteenth century, the establishment of military barracks just to the north of the suburb's environs was of massive significance. A new road grid was then laid out across much of Northgate, along with hundreds of small terraced houses built for the soldiers serving at the barracks, and their families. The names of these new streets, such as Military Road and Artillery Street, clearly reflect their origins. These many houses were subject to slum clearance from the late 1950s onwards. In fact, the changes to Northgate during this period were so drastic that I have allowed this chapter to be the largest in the book. There are also many more important Northgate photographs reserved for a second volume of *Suburbs & Surroundings*.

A fine view of the north side of Broad Street, taken near the junction with Albion Place and looking west towards the main Northgate thoroughfare. The date is 23 July 1955. Houses from the seventeenth to nineteenth centuries can be seen. Broad Street is a long road that shadows the city wall for about one-fifth of its circuit. However, it is only the short section from Northgate to Military Road that will be featured here, as part of the Northgate suburb. This section is sometimes unofficially referred to as 'Lower Broad Street'.

A fire in the upper storey of No. 78 Broad Street on 23 March 1960, taken from the junction with Northgate (Street), and looking east. At the time, this building was occupied by Frank Lyons' television and radio shop. A notice on the plate glass shop window reads, 'for one week only, any set shown here converted to L.T.A. or Rediffusion', presumably free of charge. Within minutes of this picture being taken, another fire tender would arrive and a second ladder erected to better tackle the blaze.

Nos 57 and 58 Broad Street in April 1961, marooned following the recent clearance of properties on either side. This demolition phase, which also affected some old houses in Artillery Gardens behind (see overleaf), was concerned with slum clearance and had nothing to do with the council's ring road plans, which would only have affected the buildings on the other side of the road. The 1961 residents were Reginald Belton (57, nearest the camera) and Mrs A.M. Larkin (58). The sign above No. 57 reads 'St Crispins', relating to a boot and shoe repair business since closed.

The rear elevations of other properties on the north side of Broad Street that also managed to escape demolition. These are Nos 70 to 74, a group of old houses with considerable architectural merit. No. 70 (far left) is a low-set timber-framed building, clearly of medieval origin. The loftier proportions of No. 71 next door indicate a building from the late eighteenth century. Once a grocer's shop, it had reverted to residential use by 1961. On the right are the upper-storey gables of Nos 72 to 74, dating from the 1690s. In the background is part of the King's School.

Before the slum clearance Artillery Gardens was a curious byway, part street and part alleyway, which meandered its way from Broad Street to Artillery Street. As a result, it contained old houses that faced in all four compass-point directions. Here is No. 3 Artillery Gardens, one of a pair of north-facing cottages situated in a section of alleyway and photographed during April 1958. The late 1950s resident was Vincent Franklin. Behind are the backs of old houses in Broad Street. Nos 3 and 4 were demolished in 1960.

Nos 26 to 28 Artillery Gardens, part of a west-facing terrace of six early nineteenth-century cottages, photographed in June 1960 looking forlorn, stripped out and only days from demolition. The late 1950s residents were Charles Twyman (26) and Mrs M.A. Hart (27). No. 28 had been empty since Vincent Franklin transferred to No. 3 in the early 1950s (see top picture). Following the slum clearance, a mixed development of low-rise maisonette blocks and single-storey retirement bungalows appeared across the site.

The south-facing terrace of mid-nineteenth century houses at Nos 8 (far end) to 21 Artillery Gardens, photographed in the early 1960s. This, the street section of Artillery Gardens, could be found at right-angles to the end of Albion Place. These cottages were not part of the same demolition phase that had affected the properties on the opposite page. In fact, they would last until 1968, and then be pulled down in the second-to-last slum clearance phase in Northgate, together with houses on the south side of Artillery Street behind. Today, a row of garages stands on the site.

The enchanting rear elevation of No. 7 Artillery Gardens, an east-facing cottage on the final stretch of alleyway before it joins Artillery Street. The date of this picture is 23 July 1955. On the right is the rear of No. 6, a house more typical of the area, and in the background can be seen the roofs and chimneys of properties in Artillery Street. The almost bucolic charms of this cottage were not enough to save it, and No. 7 was swept away along with the rest of the houses in the 1968 phase of demolition.

The rear elevations of Nos 77 (right) to 79 Military Road as part of a pre-demolition survey in about 1958. These properties were part of a long terrace of houses that once stood on the east side of Military Road. Note the round-topped passageway that allowed through access from the street. To the left, Mrs Short stands outside her open back door at No. 79, no doubt pondering her future. At this time, the other residents were Reuben Crawley (78) and Stephen Keeler (77).

The next section of the terrace, Nos 70 to 76 Military Road, seen from the front in April 1961. Unlike those properties in the top picture, these buildings are of simple timber-framed construction, No. 75 having a brick front elevation whereas Nos 70 to 74 had wooden weatherboarding. No. 76 (far right) is a property containing several small businesses, including Mrs Eriksson's general stores. Far left, are the walls and trees of the well-screened St Gregory's Vicarage, seemingly unwilling to look out onto its poorer parishioners.

Demolition on the east side of Military Road during December 1961. This picture was taken from almost the same spot as the one opposite. Indeed, the bulldozer is standing on an area once occupied by Mrs Short's front parlour. The wall being pulled down (right) is that between Nos 77 and 76. Soon, the bulldozer would progress as far as the vicarage and go no further. It would then move southwards, sparing only the Royal Dragoon pub at the far end. In the background are the buildings on the street's west side (see page 65).

A group of circus elephants progress slowly along Military Road, during August 1964. One can only speculate as to the conversation being held between the keeper and the bemused bicycle-mounted policeman! On the left, the aforementioned slum clearance has exposed the buildings of St Thomas' Roman Catholic School, as well as allowing it to extend its grounds right up to the street. To the right, the fizzy drinks lorry is waiting at the junction for Artillery Street.

The early nineteenth-century houses of Nos 15 to 18 Military Road, standing on the west side of the street. This picture is part of the pre-slum clearance survey of April 1958. The last residents are as follows: Miss Gibbs (15), Mrs Gold (16), Mrs Woodman (17) and Patrick O'Neill (18). As was the case with the vast majority of terraced houses across the Northgate suburb, they were originally built to provide accommodation for the families of soldiers stationed at the nearby military barracks.

The rear elevations and backyards of the same houses featured in the top picture. The original print was dated 18 April 1958, which was a Friday. Therefore, it is likely that the picture had actually been taken the previous Monday, i.e. washing day. Further along and closer to the city is a short row of newly built council houses (Nos 2 to 5 Military Road) which were the first to appear in the Northgate area. These older houses were pulled down in 1960, together with some of those in Artillery Gardens and Broad Street (see pages 58 to 61).

Nos 26 to 30 Military Road (west side) situated between the junctions for Artillery Street and Union Street, April 1961. On the far left, is the Yew Tree public house (26), run by Thomas Stephenson. Next come the homes of Joseph Amess (27) and Cyril Sunnuck (28), followed by the ice-cream maker and confectioner's shop of Miss M. Coia. On the far right is the house of Albert Terry (30). Demolition took place during 1962, in a phase that also included the south side of Union Street and north side of Artillery Street.

A rather bizarre mishap that occurred in Military Road during December 1965. The lorry carrying a vast quantity of fruit and veg has shifted its load and collided with a lamppost. This is likely to have happened on the tight bend from Broad Street into Military Road. While the unfortunate driver inspects the damage, a small group of local residents look on with interest, no doubt in eager anticipation of some free contributions towards the forthcoming family Christmas dinner. On another trivial note, the lorry is parked in exactly the same spot as the car in the top picture.

The Victoria public house at No. 70 Northgate, at the junction with St Radigund's Street, in the early 1960s. Street directories of the early 1960s do not give a proprietor's name, but in the mid-1950s it had been George Frost. The inn closed in 1966, and is now in residential use. As to the building itself, the upper-storey jettied gables indicate a late seventeenth-century date, although the pub frontage and ground-floor plaster work originate from the early nineteenth century.

An interesting section of the east side of Northgate in the early 1960s, from the junction with High Street St Gregory's (far left), right up to Broad Street (see page 58). This section of the street, on both sides, is largely characterised by three-storey buildings, with eighteenth- and nineteenth-century façades, which mostly hide older timber-framed structures behind. The photographer is standing outside the Model Tavern, another lost inn of Northgate, but in this case one that closed in the 1980s.

*Right:* Patriotic bunting and union flags being erected in Northgate on a wet day in May 1953, in preparation for the coronation celebrations. The ladder is against the Two Brothers public house, at No. 91 Northgate – an inn that would close in the mid-1960s. In 1953, the proprietor was one Mr Willey. The coronation year was also about the time when the name of this main thoroughfare was trimmed down from 'Northgate Street' to simply 'Northgate'.

*Below:* Part of the GPO sorting office complex on the corner of Northgate with Union Street, shortly after closure in 1988. Complete demolition was only a matter of months away, and this was followed by an extensive archaeological investigation to uncover and record the remains of the former St Gregory's Priory. The older building (far right) is the former Two Brothers public house. It remains today, despite demolition threats in the 1960s.

A mid-1950s view of Union Street, taken from near its junction with Military Road and looking down towards that with Northgate. The early nineteenth-century houses on the street's north side dominate, being Nos 8 right up to 38a at the top end. Note the complete absence of any vehicle, except the photographer's bicycle. This is surprising for, by the 1950s, Union Street, and part of Military Road, had taken over from much of Northgate as the main A28 trunk route into the city.

The rear of No. 30 Union Street in about 1958 when the occupant was Louvain Smith. Demolition of old houses in Canterbury ceased in 1938, because of the impending war, and slum clearance was only considered again in the mid-1950s. The first area to be chosen was the north side of Union Street and both sides of the adjacent New Ruttington Lane (see pages 70 and 71). Understandably, many owners objected to being told that their properties were 'unfit for human habitation', and any house subject to the appeals process, such as No. 30, was photographed to assist in the subsequent local enquiry.

Few, if any, objectors to a compulsory purchase order for slum clearance were ever successful, and they also had to suffer the further ignominy of having the health inspector testify as to the 'insanitary state' of their dwellings at these so-called enquiries. Therefore, it came as no surprise to anyone when demolition of the north side of Union Street began in earnest, in early 1959. The top end of the terrace is seen here from the back, with clearance work well in progress. On the left are the properties in Military Road that would be subject to similar treatment in 1962 (see page 65).

The bottom end of Military Road, near its junction with Northgate, in the early spring of 1959. About half of this void, up to the junction with Union Place, had been caused by the October 1942 blitz, but further up, slum clearance can clearly be seen to have taken place. Because of its new trunk road status, the widening of Union Street on the north side was also very much part of the redevelopment plans. Even so, East Kent decided to re-route its services along here before this had been carried out, hence the temporary bus stops, and also buses squeezing past each other in the picture.

As already mentioned, both sides of New Ruttington Lane were selected for demolition when slum clearance resumed in the mid-1950s. In fact, some of the properties on the north side of the street had already been pulled down in 1938, therefore it seemed logical to resume demolition at the same location. Pictured here are Nos 37 and 38 New Ruttington Lane, at the top of its north side, close to the Military Road junction. Despite appearances, these houses were of timber-framed construction, the front elevations being plastered over, with the rear weather-boarded.

The mid-section of New Ruttington Lane's north side in 1957. The annotation indicates that the owner of No. 53 has raised an objection to the compulsory purchase order for slum clearance. The 1950s occupant of No. 53 was Mrs Gann. The other properties are No. 48 (right) down to the corner shop at No. 55, standing at the junction with Clyde Street. Many of these houses had been empty for some time. It may even be possible that the occupants had quit prior to the late 1930s slum clearance program, which was then cancelled due to the impending outbreak of the Second World War.

The north side of New Ruttington Lane at its top end in early 1959, after much demolition had already taken place. The properties affected here are Nos 36 to 39 (two of which are featured opposite) with only the outer walls of No. 39 and the rear chimneystack of No. 38 remaining. The demolition contract for the twenty-one standing properties on the lane's north side was the first one to be awarded in the resumed slum clearance program. It went to East Kent Demolitions of Whitstable, on 5 February 1958.

The bottom end of New Ruttington Lane (north side) during the final days of demolition in early 1959. Featured here are Nos 66 and 67, standing opposite the junction with Union Place. The 1950s occupants were Alex Bennett (66) and Walter Furner (67). The small business yards in the foreground occupy the sites of Nos 60 to 65 New Ruttington Lane, which had been demolished as 'Slum Clearance Area No. 8' over twenty years before. Northgate can be seen at the far end.

Part of the east side of Northgate (Street), looking up towards the junction with New Ruttington Lane, photographed in April 1961. Featured here are Nos 124 down to 115 (right) Northgate, the last residents being L.W. Carter, hardware shop (115); J. O'Brien, horse slaughterer (120); A.J. Twyman, chimney sweep (121); Mrs Twyman (122); Mrs Gibbons (123) and Reginald Gambrill (124), nearest the camera. These nineteenth-century properties would be demolished for road-widening in late 1966. The Northgate House office block occupies the site today.

The next section along, also from April 1961 but looking in the opposite direction. Nos 125 to 127 Northgate are a row of three late eighteenth- or early nineteenth-century properties which were empty and awaiting demolition when this picture was taken. The final occupants (1955) were George Garner (125), Mrs Leaney (126) and Mrs Taylor (127). Next come a pair of houses, Nos 128 and 128a, from about 1910. By no means slums, they still would perish in late 1966 for road-widening. The final occupants were Frederick Reardon (128) and Robert Coombs (128a).

The premises of Bishop's Taxis & Coaches, on the east side of Northgate, in July 1966. It replaced the empty cottages at Nos 125 to 127, featured on the opposite page. The firm were well-established on this site by 1964. Only the front projecting wall was lost to the road-widening scheme, and the premises still survive today, being used by a car rental firm. Just seen on the left is part of the Edwardian pair (Nos 128 and 128a), then only months from demolition.

Beyond No. 128a was an area of wasteland where a row of small tenements had been demolished many years before. By the spring of 1951, lawns had been laid, borders dug, seats provided and the plot re-christened 'Priory Gardens'. The picture shows Mr C.W. Rodd, chairman of the food company Walls, and erstwhile owners handing over the new gardens to Canterbury Corporation. The deputy mayor, Cllr T. McCallum represented the council at the ceremony. The photographer is standing in a small car park established at the street frontage to Priory Gardens.

Nos 135 and 136 Northgate, in July 1966, as part of the pre-demolition survey. These cottages are of particular interest in that they date from the late seventeenth century. Note that No. 135 (right) is partly timber-framed with a jettied upper storey, whereas No. 136 is brick-built, at least at the front (see bottom picture). By the 1960s, the two cottages had become one property, owned by John Mann. To the right, is the front car park of Priory Gardens, and on the left, the gate and front wall of the Prince of Wales Youth Club.

The rear wall to No. 136 Northgate during demolition in November 1966. As can be seen, this section of the property largely consists of Caen stone blocks, re-used from a redundant ecclesiastical building. At the top of the doorjamb is a stone on which is carved 'W.S. 1687', the likely date that Nos 135 and 136 were built. The source of the stone was probably quite close by. A ruinous building, known as St Thomas' Chapel, once stood on a site now occupied by Union Street and visible remains of it still existed in the late eighteenth century. Upon demolition, the carved stone was taken to the council depot.

The side elevation of the Prince of Wales Soldiers Institute during the First World War. Dating from the 1880s or 1890s, the building was of timber-framed construction with corrugated-iron cladding on a brick plinth. The garden area (right) was situated behind Nos 135 & 136 Northgate, featured opposite. However, most people will remember this place from the 1950s and 1960s as the Prince of Wales Youth Club. Sadly, it burnt to the ground in the mid-1970s. Today, much of the site still exists, subsumed into Priory Gardens, as does part of the building's brick plinth.

Nos 137 to 140 Northgate, a short terrace of early Victorian period cottages, in July 1966. Note the tall chimneys and Welsh slate roofs. The terrace was situated opposite the junction with Kingsmead Road (note the traffic lights to the right). Also right is the low front wall and hedge of the Prince of Wales Youth Club. The last residents (1964) were John Mann (137), Mr Appleby (138), Mrs Stringer (139) and Miss Ovenden (140). Demolition occurred in late 1966.

A Fisk-Moore study of the brand new County Electrical Services Ltd premises at 141/146 Northgate, in May 1952. It was built on the site of six cottages that had been destroyed in the October 1942 daylight blitz. To the left is part of the well-known Jesus Hospital at the beginning of Sturry Road (see page 79). Finishing life as a car sales showroom, the former County Electrical Services premises were pulled down in 1988 to make way for the new Tourtel Road.

An overview of our study area from the roof of the newly-built Northgate House in June 1978. In the foreground is the flat roof of the Bishop's Taxis office, followed by the site of the demolished Nos 128 and 128a, and then the distinctive curved parking area of Priory Gardens. Next comes the site of Nos 135 and 136, followed by the gutted remains of the Prince of Wales Youth Club. Finally, after the sites of Nos 137 to 140, comes the County Electrical Services garage. As mentioned earlier, much of the open garden areas still exist today alongside Tourtel Road.

# ❧ 6 ❧

# STURRY ROAD

The Sturry Road is a continuation of the old Roman road that runs through Northgate. It follows a straight course from that suburb to the ancient village of Sturry (with Fordwich nearby), where the road splits for Herne Bay and Thanet. During the medieval period, much of the land between the road and the River Stour was owned by the Christ Church Priory (associated with the cathedral), and given over to various farming uses. As for buildings, there were a few small tenements against Sturry Road itself, and a number of water mills positioned along the river. Of these, only Barton Mill survives today, recently converted to residential use, but the oldest of the surviving buildings there do contain significant late-medieval elements. In the eighteenth century, records show that highwaymen were a problem along the quieter stretches of the road. Big changes came to Sturry Road in the early nineteenth century, at the Canterbury end, by the establishment of the military barracks on the east side, and the building of Northgate Brewery and its associated cottages and pubs on the street's west side. The barracks closed in the late 1960s, and most of its buildings along the Sturry Road frontage quickly gave way to a vast housing development. However, parts of the former Northgate Brewery have survived, in use as garage buildings, as have many of the houses and pubs built at the same time in the New Town Street area. Limited space means that only the stretch from Northgate to Barton Mill have been included this time. The rest of Sturry Road will feature in a future volume.

A somewhat careworn-looking house at No. 5 Sturry Road, situated on the west side of the street, at its Canterbury end. The picture dates from July 1966. Originally called 'Nairn Villa', the house was also once designated No. 1 Sturry Road, that is until a new No. 1 appeared in the mid-1950s (visible to the left). On the right is the entrance to Riverside Nurseries. The house was demolished in October 1975, and today the site is a small car parking area for Coldharbour Nurseries.

The vast acreage of greenhouses belonging to Riverside Nurseries, as it was in 1957. The photograph was taken from just off Kingsmead Road and looks across the River Stour. The varied buildings of Sturry Road are visible in the background. In the late 1950s and early 1960s, the nursery was run by B.R. and R.B. Henley. Today, the recently replaced coach park occupies much of the area, although a smaller business called Coldharbour Nurseries still exists off Sturry Road. In the near future, the area will change yet again as part of the Kingsmead Redevelopment Scheme.

The imposing Jesus Hospital on the east side of Sturry Road, in April 1961. Founded by a Canterbury MP in the 1590s, the hospital was originally designed to house twenty almspersons from among the city's poorest inhabitants. Of fairly simple brick construction, the building sits on a sturdy plinth of re-used ecclesiastical material, consisting of Caen stone and knapped flint. In 1933, a large extension was added (out of sight to the right). Far left is a building associated with the vast infantry barracks which, at this time, still occupied much of the east side of Sturry Road at its city end.

The Canterbury end of Sturry Road in the spring of 1988. In the foreground, a roundabout has recently replaced the traffic light-controlled junction with Kingsmead Road. Also, a short spur (right) has been built for Tourtel Road, but work on this new link did not begin until later that year. Beyond the small garage building (see page 76) is the Jesus Hospital, with the 1933 extension and also the remote warden's cottage nearest the camera.

Canterbury firemen assess the situation, having just arrived at an unusual incident at the bottom end of New Town Street, in November 1955. The frontages of Nos 19 and 20, the last two cottages on the street's north side, have collapsed into the road, also bringing the roofs down. New Town Street is a short no through road that slopes down steeply from the west side of Sturry Road, near its Canterbury end. Beyond the end houses, there is a short stretch of land before reaching the banks of the River Stour.

The men of two fire crews clear away the fallen debris in order to gain access to the devastated cottages and check for the possibility of further collapse. At this time, New Town Street had a terrace of houses on both sides. They dated from the 1840s or 1850s and were probably built in association with the almost adjacent Northgate Brewery complex. At this time, no other properties seemed affected by the subsidence which was possibly caused by a combination of the street's steeply sloping nature, inadequate foundations, and the proximity of the river.

*Right:* With regards to the occupants of Nos 19 and 20 New Town Street, luckily nobody was hurt, as the roof didn't collapse into the cottage's lower floor. This picture features the quite understandably sad and contemplative residents, Mrs M. Payne (19) and Mr and Mrs Michael Palmer (20), in the hours immediately after the incident. With repair impractical, the remains of the cottages were subsequently demolished. As to what happened to these people, the 1961 street directory lists a Mr Michael Palmer at No. 9 St Gregory's Road although there is no record of a Mrs M. Payne.

*Below:* After the incident, New Town Street settled down for another ten years, and the nettles grew on the sites of Nos 19 and 20. And then, in June 1965, the end wall of No. 18 began to collapse. In the picture, Mrs Edwards stands on the site of the lost cottages and points out the latest damage to her neighbours. In the aftermath of this further subsidence, the whole terrace on the street's north side was demolished. In addition, the bottom half of the terrace on the south side was also pulled down, leaving only the old houses at Nos 31 to 39, which still survive today.

A busy scene in Sturry Road during September 1908. A band leads the soldiers of the 7th Dragoon Guards away from the infantry barracks (right) and towards the city. They would then be boarding trains at Canterbury West station, on the first leg of their long journey to Egypt. On the left, the group of civilian onlookers are grouped around the junction for New Town Street. The Waterloo Tavern can also clearly be seen. The huge barracks complex mostly disappeared in the late 1960s, to be replaced by the Brymore Housing Estate.

The Waterloo Tavern at No. 47 Sturry Road, on the street's west side, photographed as part of Edward Wilmot's Canterbury pub survey in 1965. The building dates from the same 1840s development as the terraced houses of New Town Street, and those cottages facing onto Sturry Road adjacent to it. Once a popular haunt of the soldiers stationed at the barracks opposite, the pub is still in business today. However, it has fallen victim of the recent trend for changing pub names and is now the Run of the Mill, presumably with reference to Barton Mill.

The Black Lion pub, also from the 1965 survey, at No. 53 Sturry Road, and only separated from the Waterloo Tavern by a couple of houses. Obviously, it was assumed that there would be enough trade from the barracks opposite to justify two pubs so close together, and I'm sure they were right. However, with the barracks gone by the end of the 1960s, this no longer remained the case, and the Black Lion closed in 1969. Today, the building is a small grocer's shop, with a much-altered front and side elevation.

An interesting picture of the small single-storey grocer's shop at Nos 55/57 Sturry Road in the mid-1960s. The proprietor was Dennis E. Salter. The Black Lion pub is also clearly visible beyond. I cannot be sure when Salter's stores closed, nor when the building was demolished. In any case, it is no longer there today, and the site is part of the forecourt for Invicta Motors, who have constructed new premises behind.

Barton Mill stands at the end of the appropriately named Barton Mill Road, off the west side of Sturry Road. The accompanying photograph dates from August 1951 and shows the rarely-seen back elevations of the mill, shortly after a disastrous fire. However, unlike the other major Canterbury water mills, which met similar fiery fates, Barton Mill was subsequently rebuilt and returned to use.

The mill's more familiar front view in January 1988, a time when the River Stour had broken its banks all through the Canterbury area. Barton Mill actually stands at a location where two branches of the river merge back together again, so the flooding was particularly dramatic here. The white weather boarded section of the mill dates from the eighteenth century, whereas most of the taller structures behind appear to post-date the 1951 fire.

Barton Mill finally closed in the early 2000s, having last been used to process animal feed. By May 2003, the entire complex was empty and boarded up. The photograph shows Barton House, at the corner of Sturry Road with Barton Mill Road. This 1970s house fell within the area designated for the Barton Mill development scheme, hence its forlorn appearance here. One building definitely earmarked for retention was the lovely eighteenth-century weather boarded section, seen on the opposite page. Ironically, it was entirely destroyed by fire while awaiting conversion.

Looking down Barton Mill Road in April 2006, just after demolition of the mill complex had begun. The vast majority of the buildings seen here would subsequently disappear. Therefore, although this picture is of relatively recent date, it is no less historically valid. New buildings have since appeared across the whole site. In addition, the picturesque section of Barton Mill that fell victim to the 'fire curse' has since been skilfully reconstructed in facsimile form.

Beyond Barton Mill, a footpath leads across to Broad Oak Road, which runs parallel to Sturry Road. Featured here is a long terrace of early nineteenth-century cottages at Nos 24 to 48 (evens only) Broad Oak Road, in the late 1950s. Originally known as Nos 1 to 13 Cotton Mill Row, they had originally been built for the workforce of a long-since lost cotton mill, situated on the branch of the River Stour immediately behind them. This terrace was demolished for road-widening in the early 1960s, and now allotments can be found here.

In Canterbury's post-war development plan, much of Broad Oak Road was designated for light industrial use. The first permanent buildings began to appear in the early 1950s. This picture dates from 1953 and shows the start of construction to what would become a wholesale foodstuffs warehouse. In the background, and on the opposite side of the road, is the Central Electricity Authority Canterbury grid sub-station. In the 1960s, a new link road called Farleigh Road would be built opposite the wholesalers.

# ❧ 7 ❧

# ST AUGUSTINE'S

St Augustine's Abbey was by far the largest religious foundation established outside the city walls, and it occupied many acres of land immediately to the east of Canterbury. Much has already been written about the abbey's centuries-old history, its conversion into a Royal Palace by Henry VIII and the more recent use of the surviving buildings and land for educational purposes. As a result, this chapter will mainly concentrate on the streets and buildings that exist around the perimeter walls of this vast former abbey precinct. To the north of the study area, the streets such as Old Ruttington Lane have a similar character and history to the adjacent Northgate suburb. Further round, both Broad Street and Lady Wootton's Green have been extensively covered in my previous books, but some new pictures have come to light, and I am happy to include them here. Running along the former abbey's south precinct wall, is Longport, the site of a medieval market place (Longport meaning 'long market'). Originally, this was part of the Roman road from Canterbury to Richborough which left the city via the Burgate and Church Street St Paul's. However, in the late eleventh century, part of its course was diverted slightly to the south, in order to allow for a new lay cemetery to be positioned to the south of a vastly expanded Romanesque St Augustine's Abbey church. The original Roman course of Longport is restored adjacent to the blocked gateway known as Longport Bar.

In the late 1950s, some old terraced properties in Old Ruttington Lane were identified for slum clearance. Just like those situated on the east side of Military Road (see pages 62 and 63), the Old Ruttington Lane houses backed onto St Thomas' Roman Catholic School, so their removal would allow the school grounds to be expanded. Here we see Nos 25 and 26 on the lane's north-west side, in about 1958. Older than other adjacent properties similarly identified for demolition, this pair probably dated from the seventeenth century. Note the jettied upper-storey.

The rear elevations of Nos 25 and 26 as part of the same pre-clearance survey. Note the small rear windows and alarmingly curved chimney stacks. The mid-1950s residents were William Datlen (25) and James Barling (26). Old Ruttington Lane had fared badly in the blitz, with many of its ancient cottages being wiped out in the daylight raid of October 1942. And, because of the early post-war housing shortage, the remaining properties were much needed until the new outlying housing estates could be built in the early 1950s. Demolition occurred in about 1961.

A row of five late eighteenth-century cottages further up on the north-west side of Old Ruttington Lane, at Nos 38 to 42, April 1961. The 1955 residents were Ernest Twyman (38), Albert Burden (39), Harry Tyler (40), Thomas Roff (41) and Mrs M. Lawford (42). To the right is the rear wall to the grounds of St Gregory's Vicarage (see also page 62). Out of sight to the left is the junction for North Holmes Road. Demolition occurred in about October 1961. The ambulance station and a footpath connecting with Military Road later appeared on the site.

Looking up North Holmes Road, from the junction with Old Ruttington Lane, in the early 1960s. The work being carried out is for road-widening and the provision of footpaths on both sides, in association with the establishment of Christ Church College. This work necessitated the demolition of houses at the end of Havelock Street (right). The college, built between 1961 and 1964, can be seen in the background, partly hidden by the ancient walls that had once been associated with St Augustine's Abbey and, later, the Royal Palace.

*Left:* Lady Wootton's Green was devastated by high-explosive bombs in the Baedeker raid of 1 June 1942. The associated photograph dramatically illustrates the typical blast damage that resulted. No. 4 Lady Wootton's Green stood on the corner with Monastery Street, and is thought to have dated back to the fifteenth century. Note the twisted street sign, no doubt placed there for the benefit of the photographer. The remains of this ancient house would be bulldozed in July of the same year.

*Below:* The south side of Lady Wootton's Green, as seen from the former St Augustine's Abbey buildings in the late 1940s. As is clearly evident, no buildings on this side of the green survived the blitz and the thorough clearance operation that followed. Note that the removal of No. 4 in the foreground has allowed the corner from Monastery Street to be greatly eased. The rest of the blitzed site was used as a car park and, apparently, a short cut for vehicles cutting the corner off! Broad Street runs across the background and in front of the city wall.

Lady Wootton's Green, viewed from Broad Street in the early 1950s. Although redevelopment work has yet to be carried out, the central green area has now been neatly planted out, and a number of Canterbury citizens can be seen enjoying the surroundings. On the left is the large Georgian house of No. 1 Lady Wootton's Green, the only building on either side of the green to have survived the blitz. In the background, the former St Augustine's Abbey buildings have recently had all the wartime blast damaged repaired.

An unfortunate accident right outside the Findon Gate in March 1959. It would appear that the car's trailer had compromised its handling and so caused this disagreement with a lamppost! The south side of Lady Wootton's Green was redeveloped for housing in about 1957. Around the same time, Monastery Street was extended northwards to connect with Havelock Street. In the 1960s, the smaller gateway to the left would allow access to the new Christ Church College.

Onlookers, several people deep and on both sides of Broad Street, watch the Home Guard farewell parade in the latter half of 1944. From a vantage point atop one of the city wall bastions, the photographer has captured the moment when the second unit takes the salute as it marches past the podium. Blitz-damage along much of the east side of Broad Street is all too evident. However, a few surviving houses can be seen nearer the junction with Church Street St Paul's (right). St Paul's Church itself is also visible in the background (see page 94).

The premises of Lenfield Engineering (Canterbury) Ltd, agricultural engineers, November 1959. The building, which was situated between the east side of Broad Street, and west side of Monastery Street (behind), can also be seen to the left of the picture at the top of the page. Their impressive display of new tractors and combine-harvesters probably didn't attract much passing trade from the residents of nearby Old Ruttington Lane! Lenfield's building was demolished in the late 1960s, prior to the construction of the new law courts.

The Brewer's Delight public house at No. 33 Broad Street, in 1965. It was situated on the east side of Broad Street, between the junctions of Havelock Street (left) and Lady Wootton's Green (right). Throughout the 1950s and 1960s, the pub hardly ever failed to field teams for both the local darts and bat-and-trap leagues. The Brewer's Delight recently fell victim to the move towards the home consumption of alcohol and, at the time of writing, is undergoing remodelling for a new use.

The broad sweep of the appropriately named Broad Street in November 1966, with the low afternoon sun about to disappear behind the city wall. The Brewer's Delight pub is just out of sight to the left. Visible further up is part of the late 1950s redevelopment on the south side of Lady Wootton's Green. Beyond that, Lenfield's is still trading. The Broad Street car park (right) was opened in 1931, following the demolition of the Star Brewery. It was extended in the 1950s (nearest the camera), after the demolition of a group of old cottages.

*Above:* The junction of Monastery Street with Church Street St Paul's in the immediate aftermath of the June 1942 blitz. The St Paul's Parish Hall, alongside the church, has fallen victim to the bombing, with only the street porch left standing. On the right-hand corner, Bailey House, a doctor's surgery, has lost its upper storeys, and would soon be entirely demolished. Fortunately, the well-known late medieval range (left) survived with only minor blast damage.

*Left:* The meeting of a group of well-known Canterbury streets, during an early autumn morning in 1954. The photographer is standing on a deserted Monastery Street with the junction to Church Street St Paul's to the right, and that for Love Lane straight ahead. Longport also begins at the top end of Monastery Street. Note the white line in the centre of the street, indicating the then traffic right-of-way from Church Street and round into Longport, a route that all buses took into the city at the time. The round-cornered building is the grocer's shop of George Cross & Son.

The rear of the Canterbury Technical College & County Technical School for Boys, on the north side of Longport, in about 1948. Until 1937, these late Georgian buildings housed the Kent & Canterbury Hospital, a purpose for which they had been built. And then, during the war years, they served as an emergency accommodation and rescue centre. The ruins of St Augustine's Abbey are spread across the foreground, having been uncovered in a series of archaeological digs during the first half of the twentieth century.

The front of the Boys' Tech, partially obscured by the mature trees in its grounds, October 1965. In the foreground, although scooters don't quite outnumber the more conventional moped, they nonetheless prove that 'mod' culture had definitely arrived in Canterbury by this time! The Girls' Tech was also situated in Longport, on the opposite side, at Barton Court. The Boys' Technical School would move to new buildings off Spring Lane in the summer of 1967, and be renamed the Geoffrey Chaucer School.

A dramatic photograph taken from Longport and looking in a south-westerly direction across the narrow junction with Lower Chantry Lane. It was probably taken a few weeks after the main June 1942 raid. By this time, the streets and paths have been cleared, and barrage balloons hover over a devastated city. It is also evident that the demolition gangs have made at least one pass through the area. The building in the cente of the photograph is part of the Payne-Smith School and has already been partly pulled down, losing its gables and much of the upper storey.

A similar view from the mid-1950s, during a major street-widening programme along Lower Chantry Lane. This work would enable incoming bus routes to use the new alignment in place of the narrow, tortuous way via Monastery Street and Church Street St Paul's (see page 94). Other major trunk routes into Canterbury were earmarked for widening at the same time, including North Lane (see page 43). In the picture, the then coach park is on the right.

The much-widened junction from Lower Chantry Lane into Longport, taken from the opposite direction as those views on the facing page, December 1967. With the River Stour some distance away, this flooding can only have been the result of a ruptured water main. In the background are some of the empty outbuildings from the recently relocated Boys' Technical School (see page 95). This vast complex would hang on for a further five years, before finally being demolished in 1972. Today, St Augustine's Abbey Visitor Centre occupies part of the site.

Looking across Longport Coach Park from the bottom end of Lower Chantry Lane in about 1970. Dominating the view is the early nineteenth-century terrace of cottages called Union Row. The last residents (1967) of those houses visible here were Miss I.M. Legge (6), Donald Marsham (7), M. Weatherall and John Silk (8), Miss C. Wood (9) and Miss Todd with Miss Norris (10). The terrace was demolished in 1975 to expand the coach park, but not before a degree of protest and also occupation by squatters.

The John Smith's Almshouses at Nos 37 to 44 Longport, photographed in the aftermath of the June 1942 blitz. Sheets of tarpaulin cover the badly blast-damaged roofs, but otherwise the row hasn't come through too badly. The eight tiny single-storey cottages were built in 1657, a date that can be seen on the Flemish-style gable end, nearest the camera. In the mid-1960s, road-widening and the provision of a pavement would eliminate the small, wall-enclosed front gardens. The eight dwellings have also since been reordered into four by Anthony Swaine.

Part of the first phase for Canterbury Prison, being demolished by steel cable and bulldozer, in September 1965. Dating from 1808, this was the original gaolhouse block of what was then referred to as 'County Gaol and House of Correction'. The prison had been built opposite the Smith's almshouses, on land that had once belonged to St Augustine's Abbey. In the picture, the shape and size of the original cells can clearly be seen along the collapsing rear wall. A new reception and administration building was subsequently built on the site.

# ❧ 8 ❧

# THE NEW DOVER ROAD AREA

The area immediately to the south-east of central Canterbury does not have a clearly defined area, like suburbs such as St Dunstan's, Northgate or Wincheap. Nor does it enjoy a specific name as these other suburbs do. Therefore, I have decided to use New Dover Road as the flagship thoroughfare for this section. It is also an area covered by the splendid Oaten Hill & District Society, with the exception of Nunnery Fields, which is more appropriate to the South Canterbury chapter. New Dover Road, as well as the adjacent St George's Place, came into being during the 1790s, as one of the new turnpike roads, thus taking traffic away from the Roman Old Dover Road and the late Saxon Dover Street. Other thoroughfares in the area, such as Ivy lane and Upper and Lower Chantry Lanes, had all firmly established themselves by 1200. This south-east suburb suffered badly in the main blitz of 1 June 1942. Although this was not the main target of the Luftwaffe, the bright chandelier flares dropped over central Canterbury, just prior to the main wave of bombers, drifted in a south-easterly direction as a result of a light breeze that had suddenly developed. While this 'divine wind' undoubtedly saved the cathedral and its precincts from worse damage, many houses in the St George's Place and New Dover Road area were devastated by incendiaries and high-explosive bombs as a result.

The famous 'Hall' in Ivy Lane, as it was in the early to mid-1950s. The picture shows the place in an interim phase, i.e. after having been renovated as slums in about 1920, but before full restoration by Anthony Swaine in the late 1960s. At this time, it was still sub-divided into four dwellings (Nos 42 to 45), and demolition for slum clearance was once again being mooted. Fortunately, Mr Swaine, a long-time champion of Canterbury's stock of old buildings, ensured the hall's retention for posterity, and returned its appearance to something like its fourteenth-century origins.

Looking along Ivy Lane from its junction with Lower Chantry Lane in the spring of 1975. The hall, by now fully restored, can be seen halfway down on the left. Dominating the scene, however, is the three-storey former premises of blind makers A.H. Amey & Son Ltd, by now standing empty and awaiting demolition. Behind it, the chestnut paling fence protects the site of the recently demolished terrace, Union Row (see page 97). After Amey's had been pulled down, the coach park area was extended across the whole area of the lost buildings.

Lower Chantry Lane in the mid-1950s, looking up towards the crossroads with New Dover Road, St George's Place and Upper Chantry Lane. The junction for Ivy Lane is on the right. Work is underway to widen the lane on its west (right-hand) side (see also pages 8 and 96). The Nissen hut on the right in Ivy Lane is part of Amey's premises. Further up Lower Chantry Lane are the group of pre-fabricated huts that made up the Inland Revenue offices. Opposite, and on the corner with Edward Road, is the Doge's Chantry Café, run by Mrs Jessie Kennett.

A similar view from January 1977, but this time taken from the front garden of the Cooper Almshouses (see page 8). On the left, the corner café was still there. On the opposite side of the widened lane, the pre-fabricated 'ministry huts' had also survived, but were at this time being used by Canterbury Archaeological Trust. At the crossroads, Rutland House has since replaced a group of late Georgian houses (see page 105). During the 1980s, the prefabs would give way to a new Safeway superstore. The café finally closed in the late 1980s.

A dramatic scene in the days following the June 1942 blitz. A workman, with pickaxe, perches high atop an incendiary-gutted four-storey structure, and is about to demolish the very chimneystack upon which he is standing. A barrage balloon hovers in the sky behind him. Originally an imposing residential scheme called St George's Fields, these lofty late Georgian buildings stood on the corner of Lower Chantry Lane and New Dover Road. By the time of their destruction, they had largely been converted into offices, and designated Nos 1 to 3 New Dover Road.

A British Legion rally on a rainy day in July 1954, along the Canterbury end of New Dover Road. Behind is their headquarters, British Legion House, at No. 7 New Dover Road. Previously named The Firs and then Walton House, this large building was a lucky survivor of the blitz. The three-storey building featured in the picture at the top of this page once stood immediately to the left. Behind are some trees and a few walls at the top end of Lower Chantry Lane. British Legion House was pulled down in the late 1950s to make way for a new scheme for Caffyns.

Part of the premises of Abbott Bros Dairies at No. 15 New Dover Road during 1956. Based around an old house, this business was adjacent to British Legion House, seen on the opposite page. In the mid-1950s, Abbott Bros supplied the milk for about two-thirds of Canterbury, and here, churns are being unloaded to help meet this demand. At about the same time, the city council refused planning permission for the firm to expand their premises, on the grounds that the area was zoned for residential use. Visible opposite is Telephone House and part of Caffyns' premises.

Another British Legion parade, but this time in July 1956 and seen on the opposite side of the street. Local dignitaries take to the podium, principal among them, the Mayor Alderman Bean and his somewhat stoic-looking wife. Behind is the original garage for Caffyns Ltd, on the corner of New Dover Road and Upper Chantry Lane. In more recent years, the building became a furniture warehouse for Court's, but had to be demolished following a fire. Today, the site has been redeveloped for housing.

The brand-new extension for Caffyns Ltd, stretching along the east side of Upper Chantry Lane, in 1951. Until about 1930 this was the site of the gatehouse for Ersham House, a large mansion set back from the street and sited within extensive grounds. Little is known about this lost house, except that it had been empty for years and the gardens had become a popular play area for local children. In the picture, on the far right, is the Upper Chantry Lane entrance to the Post Office Telephones Engineering department and garage.

The interior of the newly-extended Caffyns premises in 1951, printed from a damaged negative. The original, much smaller garage had been erected by Maltby's in the early 1930s and was the first development on the former grounds to Ersham House. Other major schemes also soon occupied the site, being Telephone House and the street and houses of Ersham Road. So far, I have been unable to trace any photographs of the lost Ersham House, except for one of its demolished porch, languishing in pieces in the council depot yard.

A fascinating view of the entire west side of Upper Chantry Lane, taken from the junction with New Dover Road and St George's Place in the early 1950s. On the right is No. 26 St George's Place, a multi-occupancy building, including Roberts' Snack Bar along the Upper Chantry Lane frontage. Next is an interesting group of buildings collectively known as the 'Paddock', including stable blocks, and a three-storey Regency period house. At the far end is the Shrubbery, a larger house standing on a rounded corner plot, at the junction with Dover Street and Oaten Hill.

Another picture of the west side of Upper Chantry Lane in the early 1950s, taken in the opposite direction to the one at the top of the page. Nearest the camera, is the Shrubbery, followed by the Paddock. Even at this time, horses were being stabled here, notably those that pulled the tourist stagecoach which plied between Canterbury and the nearby coastal towns. Today, only the Shrubbery survives. All the other buildings on this side of the street were demolished to make way for the Rutland House office scheme, completed in 1971.

A fascinating glimpse through the entrance-way to Bligh Bros' Star Garage, on the south side of Dover Street, in the summer of 1959. This is part of a record of the old garage prior to its demolition and replacement by a new filling station, showrooms and office complex for Bligh's. Also to give way for the new enlarged premises were five adjacent late Georgian cottages at Nos 6 to 10 Dover Street. The new building would barely last ten years, being pulled down for an aborted office scheme. Now the site is the Dover Street exit for Holman's Meadow car park. No. 5, seen right, still exists today.

Old buildings further along the south side of Dover Street in April 1961. Left is a small, single-storey shop squeezed into a small triangular area. Without a number, the place may have once been part of Pinnock's coal merchant premises. Today, it has been converted into a house, with an upper storey added. Next come Nos 31 and 31a Dover Street, the house of Cyril Clifford and a small grocer's shop run by Mr Furlong. Originally a forge or smithy, and built round a huge chimneystack, these two small places have now been returned to being a single property. The later upper front façade has also been dismantled to reveal the original sloping roofline.

Nos 41 to 46 Dover Street, on the north side, in April 1961. Nearest the camera is the little grocer's shop at No. 46, run by F. & V. Cozens. Next door at No. 45 is the white-rendered home of Patrick Monaghan. This is followed by four empty cottages, at Nos 41 to 44. The entire terrace is of probable late seventeenth-century date, with a brick-built lower storey and timber-framed upper storey, so typical of the period. These empty properties would soon give way to an over-scale warehouse for Riceman's. This has since been converted for residential use.

The middle section of Dover Street's north side in 1988. These garage buildings had been erected for Martin Walter Ltd, whose main showrooms fronted St George's Place. They were now standing empty. Up until 1959, an oast house stood on this site, but one wall of it survived, being incorporated into the side wall of the garages at the far end. This wall became quite a talking point, as it was composed of old Caen-stone blocks, possibly salvaged from the ruins of nearby St Sepulchre's Nunnery. Sadly, the old wall subsequently perished along with the garage buildings.

A panoramic view of the east side of Oaten Hill from its junction with Dover Street in 1941. Nearest the camera is part of the shop of E. Pickersgill (Nos 3 and 4) and the tiny painted cottage of Edward Jones (5). These are of seventeenth-century origin, with nineteenth-century frontages. Next, are four mid-nineteenth-century houses (Nos 6 to 9), followed by the rendered houses of Nos 10 to 12, and finally the Regency-styled properties at Nos 13 to 15. The 1942 blitz resulted in the loss of Nos 8 to 15. The early post-war replacements were set back to allow for future street-widening.

A solemn procession makes its way along Old Dover Road on the evening of 23 September 1957. Having passed the junction of Oaten Hill, this column of clergy now turns towards the recently completed church of St Mary Bredin, situated behind the camera (see also page 113). At the procession's head is Archbishop Dr Geoffrey Fisher, who will be conducting the consecration ceremony for the new church. Just visible in the gloom are the buildings on the west side of Oaten Hill, including the Cross Keys public house, which is still open today.

# ∂ 9 ∂

# SOUTH CANTERBURY

Today, south Canterbury is best known for its prestigious housing stock, all of which is highly sought after. However, before the end of the nineteenth century, much of this area was given over to farmland, such as the orchards and fields of the former St Sepulchre's Nunnery, St Augustine's Abbey and, later, that associated with St Lawrence Farm. The farm itself was named after St Lawrence's Hospital, an ancient religious foundation whose perimeter walls can still be seen along Old Dover Road. In 1847, the Kent Cricket Ground was established within this suburb, and ninety years later the new Kent and Canterbury Hospital was built right next to it. After the war, both the Simon Langton Girls' and Boys' Grammar Schools moved to new premises built on their already established playing fields in south Canterbury (in 1951 and 1959 respectively). A third school, St Anselm's Catholic School, was also built, alongside the Langton Girls' School. The South Eastern Railway's Elham Valley Line, opened in 1889, defined the southern limits of this area for many years. However, the new Canterbury South station saw little traffic, and the new adjacent residential suburb gradually expanded in spite of its presence, not because of it. In the 1930s, the line was downgraded, just as new residential streets off Nackington Road were laid out immediately south of the line. The Elham Valley Railway finally closed in 1947, and its many line-side features have been slowly disappearing ever since.

The first of a wonderful sequence of photographs taken on Wednesday 14 July 1937. This was the day when the Duke and Duchess of Kent, Prince George and Princess Marina, came to Canterbury for the official opening of the new Kent and Canterbury Hospital off Ethelbert Road. The royal couple can be seen here upon their arrival, reviewing neat ranks of nurses in front of the new building. Note the starched, white aprons and gloves, and also the bonnets tied under each proudly upheld chin. Behind is the Archbishop Cosmo Lang, who was also patron of the hospital.

The duke and duchess were then welcomed by the president of the hospital, Mr Walter K. Whigham, on a dais specially constructed in between the two main entrances of the new building (left). Afterwards, the duke was presented with a gold key by the architect Mr Cecil Burns, and asked to 'open' the hospital with it. As well as the many invited onlookers (right), also note the unofficial sightseers in the background, making good use of the footbridge that carries the public footpath to Nackington over the Elham Valley Line.

The Duke of Kent declares the new hospital open on the balcony in front of the boardroom, with a specially constructed canopy above. Also especially built for the opening ceremony were two platforms either side of the balcony, one to house the press (on the right), the other to support the Canterbury Silver Band, nearest the camera, who provided music for the ceremony including the National Anthem. Playing in the band on this day were my grandfather Harry Crampton (euphonium) and my great uncle Bill Crampton (cornet).

The neatly hatted and suited ranks of Canterbury citizens who had managed to acquire tickets to attend the opening ceremony. Just visible, running diagonally across the seated crowd, are the nurses who had earlier been standing to attention in the first photograph. Behind the seating area are smart rows of Sea Scouts, and along the far end of the area further 'unofficial' onlookers crowded along the new earth bank in front of the railway line. This had been built up from the spoil dug out when the hospital's foundations were constructed.

*Above:* A panoramic view of the St Lawrence Cricket Ground, off the Old Dover Road, taken in the early 1950s, during Cricket Week. Ever since matches had resumed at Canterbury in 1946, crowds had been very large, as this pictures clearly testifies. Throughout Cricket Week, the city streets were often decorated with bunting, and in the grounds themselves club marquees were erected (visible to the right of the photo). On the left is the 'second' wooden pavilion of 1909. The highly regarded 'main' pavilion of 1900 is just out of sight to the left.

*Left:* Demolition in progress of two substantial late-Victorian houses, at Nos 165 and 167 Old Dover Road, in May 1984. They are one pair of a number of similar houses, some of which can be seen in the background and beyond the trees in the top picture. The demolition picture shows the properties from the rear, with the junction for St Lawrence Road just out of sight to the right. Having long-since been sub-divided into flats, the Victorian houses were being pulled down to make way for a new block of flats!

A ceremony for the laying of the foundation stone to the new St Mary Bredin Church in Old Dover Road on 31 May 1956 (see also page 108). This would be a replacement for the mid-Victorian period church in Rose Lane, which had been lost as a result of the June 1942 blitz. Behind is a terrace of late Georgian cottages at the bottom end of Nunnery Fields. The small single-storey shop at the end (partly hidden by the stack of bricks) has recently been replaced by a two-storey house. Further right are the later houses along the west side of Lansdown Road (see page 116).

A small fire in the roof of an Edwardian semi-detached house on the north side of Nunnery Road, July 1956. The photographer is standing on the junction for Zealand Road. Despite the apparently small nature of the fire, Canterbury Fire Brigade have despatched two tenders from the station, then situated near the cricket ground in Old Dover Road. Note that the right-hand tender is one of the wartime utility vehicles, still in use with the city brigade at this time.

Looking along Rhodaus Town from the top end of Watling Street in August 1955, during a veteran car rally. Beyond the familiar Invicta locomotive are three late-Victorian houses at Nos 3 to 5 Rhodaus Town, with interesting Dutch-style gable ends. They had replaced much earlier cottages which were reputed to have been built from the salvaged stone of the demolished church of St Edmund Riding Gate. The late Victorian houses were pulled down in about 1970 to make way for the Clarkson House office development. Next to the houses are the premises of Rootes Ltd.

The shining new motor fleet of John Parker & Son, steel stockholders, parked alongside their equally new buildings in the early 1960s. Parker's premises were built behind the three late Victorian cottages in Rhodaus Town, the rear elevations of which can be seen here in the background to the left. The company's tenure in Rhodaus Town proved to be short-lived, lasting barely a decade, for they also gave way to the Clarkson House office block. The impressive new Christ Church University building now stands on the site.

The fascinating premises of the Canterbury Motor Co. Ltd (later Rootes Ltd), in Rhodaus Town, during the mid- to late 1930s. Established in 1903, the car company took over existing buildings on the site, including the Canterbury Olympia Roller-Skating Rink, with its special rock maple floor. Not long after this picture was taken, the premises were modernised by the construction of a new art-deco style frontage, including showrooms (still there today) and a canopied petrol filling station.

The aforementioned canopied petrol station for Rootes Ltd in the spring of 1953, specially decorated to celebrate the coronation of Queen Elizabeth II. In fact, Rootes both decorated and repainted their entire frontage for the occasion. Many other businesses across Canterbury also proudly followed suit. This canopied forecourt, as well as the building behind, was demolished in the 1990s to be replaced by a larger up-to-date petrol filling station. Today, the original name of the 'Canterbury Motor Co. Ltd' is now back in use.

The Nunnery Tavern, at the far end of Lansdown Road at No. 30, in 1965. The road came into existence in the late 1870s as a spur off Nunnery Fields (see page 113). Lansdown Road is roughly parallel to Rhodaus Town, and is situated not too far behind it, as the crow flies. Also visible in the picture are the backs of houses in Norman Road, situated on the other side of the railway line. The pub closed in 1968, and is now a private dwelling.

A coach derailed on points during shunting manoeuvres at the 'Dover' end of Canterbury East station in September 1955. The picture has been taken from the footpath that links Lansdown Road with Rhodaus Town and Station Road East. From this view, it is unclear if the E1 locomotive No. 31509 has been summoned to assist, or had caused the accident in the first place. Behind and to the left, are the new council houses of Oxford Road, in an area between south Canterbury and Wincheap, known as Martyr's Field.

Beret- and cap-wearing children, together with some surprisingly cheerful-looking mothers, wait on the Down platform of Canterbury East station for the evacuation trains, in September 1940. However, what seems to have attracted the cameraman's attention is the poignant sight of a teddy bear atop a small suitcase. The destination for many Canterbury children would be South Wales, although during the same month, half of the Simon Langton Girls' School was evacuated to Reading. In October 1940, half of the Boys' School went to Wantage in Oxfordshire.

An evacuation train heads out of Canterbury East station, seemingly in the wrong direction, on the same day in September 1940. Once again, an air of cheerfulness seems to be the prevailing mood. Note the ice-cream man on the platform.
I wonder how much business he did that day! Ironically, as the Second World War was declared, Canterbury became a reception area for children being evacuated from London and the Medway towns. However, the ever-increasing threat of invasion in early 1940 bought about a rapid re-evaluation of this policy.

A wartime picture of a largely deserted Canterbury East station, taken from the 'London' end of the Up platform. Of special interest is the complete covering which not only extends across both platforms but also covers both tracks. This was a common practise at many of the larger stations in the golden age of steam. One can only imagine what it was like being in there on a windy day! By the early 1950s, the Canterbury East station covering had become a rusting metal skeleton, and its days were numbered.

April 1959 and the first electric train, on a test-run from Faversham, glides into platform one of the East station. The photographer is standing in almost the exact location as in the picture at the top of the page. The electric third-rail had already been in place for some months, but by the end of May 1959, the days of steam traction on this particular line would be numbered. Note the group of trainspotting schoolboys watching the arrival. The train itself is a two-car, semi-fast unit, designated 2-HAP and numbered 6039.

# ❧ 10 ❧

# WINCHEAP

Wincheap was originally established as a linear suburb along the old Roman road from Canterbury to Lympne that left the city via the Worth Gate, and later the Wincheap Gate after the castle precincts had been closed to through-traffic. The suburb's name comes from its origins as a wine or wagon market, and the wide section of main street near the Canterbury end, gives further evidence as to this use. A number of large houses and inns had been established on both sides of Wincheap by the fifteenth century, with several small spurs off the main thoroughfare containing tiny tenements. Elements of these late medieval buildings still survive today. The arrival of the London, Chatham & Dover Railway in 1860, and the consequent construction of the iron overbridge (as well as embankment on either side of it), effectively severed Wincheap from the rest of Canterbury. This sense of isolation was further emphasised by the construction of the ring road across Wincheap Green a hundred years later. The Elham Valley Railway bridge further divided the suburb in 1889, but its presence proved to be short-lived, and demolition occurred in 1955, some eight years after the line had closed. The suburb of Wincheap really came into its own in the last quarter of the nineteenth century when Dane John Manor was sold, and a network of new streets with such patriotic names as Tudor, York and Victoria Road were laid out across the former farmland. Shortage of space means that only the section of the suburb between Wincheap Green and Victoria Road will be covered in this chapter, but the remainder will be featured in a future volume.

Wincheap Green is that part of the suburb situated between the city wall and the Canterbury East railway line approaches. Seen here in 1960 are Nos 32 to 36 Castle Street, with the narrow junction to Wincheap Grove on the left. On the right is the truncated city wall, with Canterbury Castle beyond it. Wincheap Green would be drastically altered by the construction of the Rheims Way in the early 1960s, and all the cottages in this picture were demolished. The last residents were Albert Longland (32), Mrs Benge (33), Leslie Dale (34), Phillip Coombs (35) and Arthur Sutton (36).

On the opposite side of Castle Street, and at its junction with Wincheap Green, was the Castle Hotel (No. 30 Castle Street), a mock-Tudor establishment which had replaced the earlier 'Victoria Inn' in about 1900. It is pictured here in September 1961. Just visible to the left is the former Sessions House at No. 28. Right are the transport café of R. & V. Green at No. 1 Wincheap Green, and the wholesale newsagents of A.T. Friend (No. 2). As for the Castle Hotel, proprietors William and Ethel Lack finally shut up shop in January 1963. The place was demolished only days afterwards.

The route of the new ring road, with construction well underway, towards the end of 1962. The pipes in the foreground are lying on the site of Nos 32 to 36 Castle Street, seen on the opposite page. The terraced houses of Wincheap Grove had also gone by this time. On the left are the garages to the rear of the BRS depot, and also the recently completed warehouse of F. Friday & Son – wholesale distributors of agricultural produce (also known as fruit and veg!). The city wall, on the far right of the picture, provides a useful point of reference.

An aerial view of the whole Wincheap Green area from October 1980. By this time, Wincheap roundabout had been in existence for some seventeen years, linking stages one and two of the city ring road. On the far right are the castle and former Sessions House, by this time both situated right at the top end of Castle Street. The depots of BRS and Friday & Son are also again seen, in the top half of the photo. Nearer the bottom is part of Canterbury East station (see also page 118), with Gordon Road to its left.

Looking along the Canterbury end of Wincheap in August 1964, from just beyond the railway bridge that carries the line into Canterbury East station. An East Kent bus approaches on the city route No. 24 from Thannington to Sturry Road. It is about to traverse that part of the road that had been specially lowered to allow traffic enough room to pass beneath the aforementioned bridge. Next to the bus on the right is the Maiden's Head public house of fifteenth-century origin. Just beyond is a recently cleared area that would soon become the site for a widened Simmonds Road (see page 124).

The shops and buildings on either side of the Tudor Road junction, on the south-east side of Wincheap, in the late 1960s. Far left is the early 1950s extension to the BRS repair centre. At the corner with Tudor Road is the substantial nineteenth-century building at No. 21 (formerly 185) Wincheap, encompassing the Spar grocers, with living accommodation above. On the opposite corner is the small house of George Attwood (23), with its steeply-pitched roof indicating a probable seventeenth-century date. Far right is the Eastman's butcher's shop, at No. 25 (formerly 183).

*Right:* The next narrow junction on the south-east side of Wincheap, is that for York Road, pictured here in the 1920s. Nearest the camera are Nos 177 and 178 Wincheap – two large town houses built in the second quarter of the nineteenth century. On the opposite corner is a pair of older buildings of likely late sixteenth- or early seventeenth-century date, at Nos 179 and 180. Note the first-floor jetty and steeply pitched roof, indicating a largely timber-framed structure. No. 179, right on the junction, would be converted into a shop during the 1930s, and a 'modern' shop front imposed.

*Below:* A scene of utter devastation further up York Road as a result of the sudden daytime raid of Saturday 31 October 1942. High-explosive bombs have wrecked houses on both sides of York Road and near its junction with Grove Terrace. Nearby buildings fronting the main Wincheap Street were also levelled. All badly damaged houses in York Road and Grove Terrace were soon cleared away, and later replaced by modern terraced housing with small front gardens. The blast-damaged houses in Grove Terrace, visible in the picture, were subsequently repaired and survive today.

The newly-opened premises of Pilgrim Cycles at Nos 17 and 18 Wincheap, on its north-west side, June 1960. The building started life as two terraced houses, built in about 1810, and had been a greengrocer's shop before Pilgrim Cycles took over. As can be seen, they also traded in mopeds and scooters, both of which were extremely popular at the time. Left is the narrow junction into Simmonds Row (see the page opposite). On the right is the empty house at No. 16, apparently being used as a cycle store by the firm.

The Pilgrim Cycles business didn't last long. As is evident in this dramatic picture from April 1962, a devastating fire completely gutted the premises. The blaze, attended by at least two fire crews, also spread along the open roof space of all the adjacent properties to the right. Therefore, also affected by it were Frank Marsh, cooked meat store (14), and Louis Preen, fishmonger (15), as well as the empty house that Pilgrim Cycles had been using. Having stood empty for a short period, the entire terrace was demolished in advance of the widening of Simmonds Row.

Looking down Simmonds Row from its junction with Wincheap, probably in the 1920s. In all likelihood, these terraces were built in the same 1810 scheme as the similar houses on either side of the junction and fronting Wincheap. On the left of the picture are Nos 1 to 9 Simmonds Row, with Nos 10 to 17 situated opposite. At this time, there was more than one member of several families living here. For example, Mr Henry Joy lived at No. 3 with Mrs Joy at No. 4. Other examples are Alfred Bundock (6), Edward Bundock (7), Miss Hart (8) and Mrs Hart (13).

Nos 10 to 17 (right to left) Simmonds Row in March 1967, all empty and awaiting demolition. The left-hand terrace had been chosen for slum clearance in the late 1930s, but not demolished until the late 1940s when a row of lock-up garages were built on the former back gardens. At the same time, Nos 10 to 17 were renovated for further use, with rendered walls and new roofs. However, by 1965 the city council had identified the area as the site for a new industrial estate, so had the terrace condemned. Simmonds Row was then widened to become Simmonds Road.

*Left:* The small Sportsman public house on the south-east side of Wincheap at No. 79 (formerly 160), photographed as part of Edward Wilmot's pub survey in 1965. The pub is the end property of an early to mid-nineteenth-century terrace situated between Biggleswade's Passage and Underdown's Passage, the latter of which is visible to the right of the picture. The pub closed in 1969 to become the Sportsman Café, a role it still fulfils to this day.

*Below:* Nos 1 to 4 Underdown's Passage, a terrace of probable eighteenth-century date, photographed in about 1967. The cottages were situated behind the Sportsman pub, and only a few yards along the passage on its north-east side. At this time, the occupants were Mr L.F. Foulser (1), Sidney Harris (2), Miss Cox (3) and Mrs Amos (4). The date of demolition is uncertain, but it is likely to have occurred by 1975. Today, Underdown's Passage has been greatly truncated, and no longer extends to the sites of the lost cottages.

*Right:* The Duke's Head public house, on the north-west side of Wincheap at No. 29, photographed as part of the 1941 survey. The proprietor was one Edwin Hitchlock. Note the building's hipped roof with gablet at the top, which indicates a structure of fifteenth-century origin, and although much altered over the years, the building still contains medieval elements as part of its fabric. The pub closed in 1972 and is now a private dwelling at No. 62 (in the early 1960s renumbering). It is also interesting to note that the horizontal beam that once supported the pub sign is still in place today.

*Below:* A fine double-fronted, mid-seventeenth-century house at No. 33 Wincheap, also pictured by Mr Fisk-Moore for the 1941 building survey. Note the double-jettied frontage, with a fine set of carved corbel brackets. It is also interesting that at the time this photo was taken, the place was being offered for sale as an 'interesting Tudor residence'! Sometimes known as Wincheap House, the last private resident was George Green. The post-war years saw a number of businesses trading from here, and in more recent years it has been an Indian restaurant.

Camels and elephants are not an everyday sight in Wincheap. However, on one particular day, sometime in the 1890s, drinkers from the Duke's Head and Sportsman must have all rubbed their eyes in disbelief. In reality, this magnificent parade is a collection of exotic animals and equally exotically dressed employees of Barnum & Bailey's Circus. Behind the camels, neatly pollarded trees partly hide Wincheap House, featured on the previous page. Adjacent to the elephant are two ancient dwellings, which would give way to Blundell's Tyre Service premises in the 1950s.

A final look back along our Wincheap study area in August 1964. The signs of the Sportsman pub can just be seen on the right, while further down, and on the opposite side of the street, are the trees in the side garden of No. 74 (formerly No. 33). Also worthy of note are the substantial chimney stacks of the three-storey villas at Nos 84 to 90 (evens only), built in the 1880s. This is the widest stretch of Wincheap, a legacy from the old market days, but this does little to ease today's traffic problems because of the bottlenecks at either end of it.